Critical Praise For
No Sneakers at the Office

This is the ultimate mentorship resource. It allows young people
to be optimally successful in business sooner, while avoiding the
pitfalls and career traps of older generations. This wealth of wis-
dom gives readers the competitive edge in a constantly changing
business environment. As a product of enlightened mentorship
myself, I honor Adam T. Scholl for this definitive work.

—**Hank Moore,** Corporate Strategist™
Author of the best-selling *Business Tree*™,
Growth Strategies and Tactics for Surviving and Thriving

A quick skim of *No Sneakers at the Office* and you may wonder
why anyone would need a book of such obvious advice. But dig
deep   perfect
fect   an-
age   ght
and   to
exc

Y

Th   er
the   ti-
cal   ve
you

nt

no
Sneakers
at
the
Office

no
Sneakers
at
the
Office

A Practical Handbook
for the Business World

Adam T. Scholl MBA, JD

LANDMARC
P R E S S

Acknowledgments

I would like to thank Evan Peterson, MBA, JD, for his tireless feedback, constructive criticism and support in bringing this work to fruition. When I first approached Evan for his assistance, he instantly agreed and began helping with research, editing, and project management. I am especially grateful for his constant encouragement throughout the creative process.

Contents

no
Sneakers
at
the
Office

INTRODUCTION

It's better to hang out with people better than you. Pick out associates whose behavior is better than yours and you'll drift in that direction.

—WARREN BUFFETT

WHO I AM

I was born in New York in
May of 1975 and spent my
youth growing up in Illinois,
Utah, and Florida. After high
school, I entered the Florida
Army National Guard and
continued my education
at community colleges. I
received my bachelor of
science in Management

Information Systems from Florida State University
in August 2000. I accepted a position with Publix
Super Markets, Inc.—a *Fortune 500* company—as a
programmer in October 2000. The following year, I
began the master of business administration program
at Saint Leo University, receiving my MBA in August
2003. During my subsequent five and half years
at Publix Super Markets, I held multiple positions
including numerous leadership roles. I not only grew
as a software engineer, manager, and leader, but also as
a professional.

While I continued to progress in my career at Publix Super Markets, I had the opportunity to co-produce
and co-direct the documentary film *Agent Orange: The
Last Battle,* which was released in late 2004. The film

illustrated the plight of two Vietnam veterans (Richard and Tony) who were dealing with life after being exposed to agent orange. The victims recounted stories of being sprayed and how they survived one war only to find themselves fighting another one—the battle against the effects of agent orange. An unexpected result of the film was that thousands of Vietnam veterans received help in fighting the effects of this chemical.

After obtaining my MBA, releasing the documentary film, and progressing successfully within my career, I decided that I needed to further expand my skill sets. I realized that it was important to have a good grasp of the legal system. Moreover, I knew that I wanted to improve my writing, oratory, and analytical skills so I decided to attend the University of Detroit Mercy School of Law in the fall of 2006.

I prepared myself before entering law school but I also thought that I might have an easy time in a professional school because of my age and experience—I was sorely mistaken. My rude awakening took place on the first day of class when I was re-introduced to the Socratic method of teaching. Being the first person *volunteered* to articulate the specifics of the first legal case was no easy task. However, I persevered and adapted. I realized during the first summer of law school while working at a Fortune 1000 corporation as a business system analyst that my love for business had not faded and that I needed to return to the corporate world once I graduated.

After three years of law school, I was ready to get back into the business community; however, my graduation came during one of the worst economic downturns of the past century. Career positions in the corporate world were bleak. The unemployment rate was hovering around 10 percent nationally. However, because of my experience, I was able to wait for the perfect position with another Fortune 500 company.

I am enjoying being back in the corporate world. My new position and corporation were the right choice for me. I wake up each day happy to go to work; moreover, I am being challenged on many levels. I look forward to the future because I own and control my career path.

WHY I WROTE THIS BOOK

I was sitting among my fellow law school graduates on May 8, 2009, waiting to accept my diploma and contemplating my future plans when I looked down and noticed something peculiar: sneakers. Yes, despite the prestige and ceremony surrounding this significant event, many of my fellow graduates had not even bothered to wear dress shoes. Some even wore flip-flops and Chuck Taylor All-Stars. With all the grooming and preparation that we had received for entry into the professional world, they still lacked the wherewithal, or the concern, to put on an appropriate pair of dress shoes. Was this the kind of professionalism one would expect from individuals about to enter the legal profession? Not even close.

The incident reminded me of the beginning manuscript for this book, which I initially started writing prior to attending law school. Bogged down by other commitments and activities, however, I'd filed the manuscript high up on a shelf in my closet. Yet, what I'd just witnessed made me realize that the book I had started to write was needed now more than ever, especially with today's fiercely competitive job environment. I knew that I had to finish and publish this book because the goal of this book is to provide individuals new to the corporate environment with the tools—business practices and principles—that will enable them to successfully manage their first few years.

The business practices and principles that I discuss in this book are based on the experiences and knowledge I gained during my six years in the corporate world and my formal education. I was fortunate enough to begin my career at a respected and distinguished major corporation, Publix Super Markets, Inc. Publix allowed me to develop my skills within the context of a first-rate corporate environment, which is indispensable for growth as a young professional. In addition, I had the steadfast and unconditional support of my parents. Equally important, I found several de-facto mentors within Publix who helped me in many ways—thank you Jim Cardenas, Stephanie Jobe, Shane Johnson, Arindam Sabui, and Chris Sykes.

Because these initial years of my odyssey into the corporate world were some of the most memorable of my life, I want to share my own experiences and unique wealth of knowledge with you—the new professionals who are just starting odysseys of your own. It is my hope that you will benefit from the insight and tips of someone who has recently walked in your shoes (not sneakers!).

HAVE THE RIGHT ATTITUDE

Let's begin with something that you should keep in mind at all times when reading this book and starting your career: **Attitude is everything.** There is no substitute for having the right attitude. You should be extremely proud of what you have accomplished so far, whether it consists of graduating from college and securing your first professional position, or rising through the ranks of your company through years of determination and dedicated service.

By the same token, however, do not let this pride cloud your judgment and delude you into thinking that you know everything. Resolve right now to face the harsh realization of how little you actually know. Although this concept may seem like common sense, and although it may be a slogan nearly as old as the printed word itself, the reason this notion now probably drives you mad is because it is true.

The corporation that has hired you believes you have the *basic* knowledge and ability to be shaped and molded into what it considers a productive asset. Your employers realize that you do not *yet* have the vast wealth of knowledge that will add to its bottom line. However, they believe, correctly, that you have great potential and that you will begin to amass a wealth of knowledge and prove to be an invaluable member of the team as your career unfolds.

Therefore, it is necessary that you realize the difficult truth, right now, today, that you do not know everything. None of us do. However, this book, along with your coworkers, other books, lectures, on-the-job training, and work experience, will assist you in becoming a better employee and a vital asset to the corporation. As a result of your time and efforts, you will experience nothing but success in your future career.

Are you ready to start amassing the tools that will enable you to reach your potential? Let's get started!

CHAPTER 1

THE CORPORATE LOOK

The quality of a leader is reflected in the standards they set for themselves.

—Ray Kroc

CHAPTER CONCEPTS

The Importance of the
Corporate Look

Possible Negative Judgments
Due to Improper Dress

How to Look Corporate

Business Formal Attire

Business Casual Attire

Casual Day Attire

General Don'ts

THE IMPORTANCE OF THE CORPORATE LOOK

It is extremely important that you have the proper corporate look. You want to be remembered for your work, NOT your attire. If your style of dress does not mesh with that of your corporate environment, then your coworkers and superiors could develop a less-than-desirable impression of you.

As it is, you will need to overcome a multitude of other obstacles in order for your work to be reviewed fairly and objectively. Don't make things any harder than they already are by adding questionable attire to the equation, especially when a professional and well-manicured appearance is so easy to achieve with just a little common sense.

Moreover, in this fast-paced work environment professionals have to make quick decisions that are based in part on judgments. And judgments are derived from one's experience and perceptions. But these judgments are used daily to make decisions on whether to promote an employee, to provide an employee an opportunity to showcase his or her talents in front of customers and so on. This is why it is important to have the proper dress so that your managers and coworkers alike do not create a negative judgment of you based upon your clothing.

POSSIBLE NEGATIVE JUDGMENTS DUE TO IMPROPER DRESS

- You are not a team player.
- You are unwilling to comply with the standards of corporate America.
- You believe this is a job—not a career.
- You do not embrace change.
- Your work is messy.
- You are not trustworthy.

These are just a few possible negative judgments your management and coworkers may have of you because of your improper dress. By dressing properly you can make certain that they do not have these negative judgments; moreover, it will also showcase your professionalism and awareness of the importance of the corporate look. Hence, having the corporate look allows for your work to be showcased instead of judgments being made about you.

HOW TO LOOK CORPORATE

It is relatively easy to obtain and maintain the corporate look. From our everyday life experience, we have already learned many of the fundamentals of how to achieve a professional look. However, it is still important to review these basics along with other components of the corporate look because some of these principles are slightly different for the nonbusiness environment.

This chapter has been divided into the following four sections:

- Business Formal Attire
- Business Casual Attire
- Casual Day Attire
- General Don'ts

> *Follow the guidelines in your company's dress code policy.*

BUSINESS FORMAL ATTIRE

Business formal attire is the dressiest attire that you will be required to wear. The primary component of this style of dress is the business suit—yes, this applies to women too. Specifically, the business formal attire for men and women is comprised of a business suit, which includes a jacket, shirt/blouse, tie for men, and pants or skirt; equally important, a dress is also appropriate for women as long as it projects the level of professionalism that one would expect of business formal attire.

Business formal attire is not intended to make you uncomfortable all day, but rather to show that you are a professional who should be taken seriously. You could very well find yourself dressing in business formal attire when meeting with external or internal clients, representing your organization in off-site functions, conducting interviews, and at other similar functions.

> *Dress for the position that you want not the position that you have!*

Remember, you also need to review your corporate policy to determine if deviation from this list is allowed (or even required). If you are unsure, don't hesitate to ask your managers and mentors. The following is a list of the basics of business formal attire:

- The business suit and dress should be neutral in style and color.
- Wear a shirt/blouse that is white or lighter in color—no patterns.
- Ensure that your tie is neutral in color and not overwhelming in its patterns.
- Employ conservative hairstyles and makeup.
- Be conservative with your accessories.

- Shoes should be polished and buffed and cover your entire foot.
- Men, your belt needs to match your shoes and your socks need to match your pants.
- Proper grooming includes a clean shave for men.

PERSONAL ACCOUNT

I remember one meeting with a company that wanted to sell us an expensive product. When I walked into the meeting room, one of the engineers from the company stood up and walked over to shake my hand. I noticed very quickly that this young man had pants on that were probably five inches too short because I was blinded by his bright white socks. Moreover, he was wearing a clip-on tie. His appearance distracted me and made me wonder why he was dressed that way; equally important, I could not understand why the people sitting next to him would let him dress in a manner that would distract potential customers. After the meeting, my coworkers and I spent time talking about this young man's attire rather than the presentation. You want to be remembered for your presentation, not your bright white socks and clip-on tie.

BUSINESS CASUAL ATTIRE

It is likely that you will be wearing business casual attire on a routine business day. This category of business dress is not as strict as business formal, so it is not necessary that you wear a full suit. However, it does requires you to wear wrinkle-free shirts/blouses and pants or skirts. It is still necessary to dress in a manner that allows you to work comfortably while still being taken seriously as a professional member of the corporate team.

The following list is a guideline for business casual attire; however, check your corporation's dress code policy to be sure you understand its requirements.

Wear

- Pressed dress pants, khakis, or skirts that are neutral in color and style.
- Neutral (in color and style) pressed shirts or blouses (women) and collared shirts that are wrinkle-free with a white T-shirt underneath (men).
- Shoes that are polished and that cover your feet.
- Conservative hairstyles and makeup.
- Limited, tasteful accessories.

- A belt that matches your shoes and socks that match your pants (men).

- Again, proper grooming (which includes a clean shave for men).

> Keep an extra long-sleeve shirt or blouse at your desk in case of an emergency.
> Trust me, there will be numerous times when a disaster will strike. Having an extra shirt or blouse will defuse the damage.

CASUAL DAY ATTIRE

Many corporations now have one day of the week when employees can dress down from the business casual standard. This day is supposed to allow employees to have a more relaxed feeling. However, it is still a business day. As such, most companies that have a casual day will have policies stating the guidelines for casual day. So again, it is very important that you review your corporation's policy.

> Casual day is not a license to
> wear anything you want!
> You are STILL at work!

Equally important, due to the dynamic nature of the business world, companies are forced to react very quickly when new circumstances and problems arise. As a result, it is not unusual for clients and bosses to schedule impromptu meetings when issues need to be resolved immediately. And, yes, sometimes these events occur on a casual attire day. The last thing you want to do is show up at the meeting wearing a logoed T-shirt—another good reason for that spare shirt in your desk drawer. Ensure that you dress for success even on casual attire days. Casual usually means no tie, no jacket.

Casual attire day is intended to allow employees to have a more relaxing dress day not a relaxing work day. T-shirts, sneakers, shorts, sandals, tank tops, stylish shirts, or pants, and so on are not okay items to wear on casual day. You want your work to be showcased not your dress. Remember that you want to be a leader not a follower. Dress for the position you want—not the position that you have.

GENERAL DON'TS

The previous discussion provided the basics for achieving and maintaining the corporate look in any situation that the business environment will throw at you. Please remember, however, that you always want to follow your company's attire guidelines. These company-specific requirements will likely be listed in your company handbook. If they are not, take time to talk with mentors and coworkers to be sure you understand the ground rules. Make no mistake, even if they are not written, they exist and you need to learn them.

This section was developed from the many instances of do's and don'ts that I have seen in my career; and the many do's and don'ts that I continue to see on a daily basis. However, there is one story that I believe will convey the essence of this chapter.

Personal Account

There was a new contractor who was hired to assist our company in developing a new product. This contractor was competent and productive; however, this person had tattoos on his arms that were very colorful and unique. These tattoos became a distraction because this person wore short-sleeved shirts. Management questioned his professionalism because he did not make an effort to cover up the tattoos. When the contractor wanted to be put on another project that would require him to interact with other business units, his request was denied because of his appearance. Even though this contractor was competent, he did not appreciate that his appearance affected his ability to interact with other units in the corporation.

Contractor

A contractor is a person who is hired for a specific period of time for a specific task. Most contractors have a contract term of six months or one year, which means their loyalty to the company is limited to the time frame of their contract.

Consultant

A consultant is a person who is hired to provide expertise in a particular matter. A good consultant will also be a well-rounded business person.

While it is very important to follow the principles outlined in this chapter, it is equally important, perhaps more so, that you are also aware of things that you should avoid at all times when trying to maintain the corporate look. Some things to avoid include:

- **Tattoos.** Tattoos should *never* be visible in the corporate setting. This encompasses off-site trips, office parties, events, business trips, and so on. You do not want your business associates to remember you because of a tattoo.

- **Too much skin.** Your clothing should never expose your chest, cleavage, shoulders, stomach, or a large portion of your thighs.

- **Piercings.** Ladies, piercings should never be visible any place other than on your *lower* earlobe for earrings. Gentlemen, you should *never* wear earrings, period!

- **Controversial clothing.** Clothing should never convey political, religious, or any other controversial matters. In addition, *never* wear clothing that is faded or torn. Equally important, under no circumstances should any undergarments ever show. Last, your clothing should never be too tight.

- **Inadequate grooming.** Facial hair is not appropriate, including beards and goatees. If you must have a beard for religious or medical reasons, then ensure that you keep it neat and trimmed. Furthermore, never allow nose or ear hair to be visible to others. Last, ensure that you have a conservative hairstyle.

- **Poor hygiene.** Regardless of your gender, you cannot allow your fingernails to become excessively long or dirty. Your hands should be clean and neatly groomed at all times. Last, be careful that your breath is not offensive to others. If you smoke, use a breath spray or drops. Never eat raw onions at a business lunch. There is *no* way to neutralize your breath after raw onions or garlic.

Keep a small mirror in your desk to ensure that your face and teeth are not dirty.

IN CLOSING

This chapter can be summed up by the old adage *dress for success*. It is that simple. You are dressing in the manner that is proscribed by your profession so that you have an opportunity to showcase your work product. Moreover, deviating from your company's dress code results in unwanted attention that is not needed in your career. This is why it is easy and important to know the types of attire that your profession expects. Equally important, you want to always be dressed for the position you want. Dressing appropriately is easy and important so there is no reason not to do it. Remember, this is a career—not a job—so treat it as such.

2

PROFESSIONALISM IN COMMUNICATION

The more elaborate our means of communication, the less we communicate.

—JOSEPH PRIESTLEY

CHAPTER CONCEPTS

You Are Your Work

Creating Professional Work

Principles of Professionalism

Corporate Memos

E-mail

Phone Etiquette

Business Presentations

YOU ARE YOUR WORK

The quality of your work is a reflection of who you are so it is important that your work always be professional. Your work affects your team and your work assignments, promotions, pay raises—everything in your professional life. By always creating and delivering the highest quality work, you will not have to worry about negative prejudgments.

Although it might seem unfair, prejudgments are common and necessary in the workplace because managers must make choices about which employees are willing and able to perform the tasks essential to the company's success. By controlling the quality of your work, you are also controlling how others within the company perceive you. As a result, professional work usually enables professional success.

CREATING PROFESSIONAL WORK

As you begin your career in the business world, you will need to communicate through multiple channels to clearly and effectively convey your message to your team, coworkers, customers, and superiors. For example, any discussion between yourself and a coworker about a given job task is considered to be work and is part of your job. As such, your oral communication with that coworker *must* be professional. Professionalism in this context is accomplished by using proper English, staying on topic, showing respect, listening as well as talking—myriad things that you must be aware of and that you must control.

E-mail has developed into one of the most important and prevalent forms of workplace communication. However, because it is so easy to communicate through e-mail, this has led some people to believe it is acceptable and appropriate for an e-mail message to contain no salutation, poor grammar, run-on sentences, or no sentences at all. This lack of professionalism has absolutely no place in the corporate world because an e-mail message is just as much your work product as anything else. When you stop and consider it, the only difference between an e-mail message and a company-wide memorandum is that an e-mail is a form of instant communication. Think of it this way: If you would not do something in a memorandum, then you should not do it in an e-mail.

E-mail and memoranda are examples of two of the many channels of communication that you must utilize to effectively perform your job. The realization that you are constantly being observed and judged by how you communicate with others can be very intimidating, especially as you are just beginning your career.

However, it is easy to overcome your anxiety as long as you always remember to be professional when conveying your message. If you always follow that simple rule, then you will gain credibility and respect among your fellow employees and become known as an individual who always acts in a professional manner.

Creating professional work is both difficult and complicated, and it requires continuous development. In other words, the further you progress along your career track, the more the quality of your work will need to improve. That means you will have to constantly augment your strengths and overcome your weaknesses. As a personal example, the more I progressed in my own career, the more evident it became that I needed to improve my writing skills. I realized that my writing skills, as they existed at the time, were insufficient given my desired professional goals. I decided to attack this obstacle, along with a few others, by attending law school. I am not suggesting that to become a better writer you must attend law school. Rather, I am suggesting that you must take control of your career and decide what you want and how to achieve it. For me, law school provided a way to improve a number of skills that I felt needed development. Self-improvement goes hand-in-hand with this reflective process.

There are some basic principles for creating professional work that should habitually apply to all forms of communication. A word of caution: While these principles provide an excellent foundation, it is up to you to modify, adapt, and evolve as you progress in your career. Just as your career is dynamic and ever evolving, so too are these principles.

BASIC PRINCIPLES OF PROFESSIONALISM

- Use proper grammar when writing and speaking.
- Listen/read before you speak/write.
- Address all people with respect.
- Do not guess; just state all relevant facts.
- Be on time with all work.
- Conform to all corporate communication standards.
- Be respectful of others' beliefs and feelings.

These principles are the building blocks that you can use to create professional work. In the sections that follow, I provide more in-depth and detailed information on how to use these principles to create a professional work product. So that you can easily reference this information in the future, I have broken it down into different segments based on the different forms of communication. Carefully review and utilize the information provided in the following sections because it will allow you to outshine the rest.

CORPORATE MEMOS

Corporate memos is a broad category that includes all written communication, except e-mails, intended for internal and external use. Even though this category encompasses many types of memos, such as *Requests for Proposals, Return on Investment* memos, *Statement of Work* documents, and so on, there are certain basic principles that can be applied to all corporate memos.

Template. A template is an extremely useful tool that can save you a great deal of time and anxiety, especially when you are on a deadline. Although choosing the exact formatting and style guidelines is largely a matter of your personal preference, any template you decide to use should contain at a minimum the following pieces of information:

Name, Title

Date

Department

Names/Titles of Recipients

Project title/Number

Issue

Proposal

Analysis

Conclusion

Format. When formatting your document, it is important to use the same font size and style throughout the entire body of the document. Headings should be a different size or style to make them stand out, but make sure that any variations you make to the headings are kept consistent throughout the entire document.

Keep the following helpful tips in mind when formatting your documents:

- Use Times New Roman and a size 12 font.
- Number your pages.
- Include headings for each new topic.
- Do not try to be witty or sarcastic.

Spelling and Grammar. When creating your document, be sure that you pay extra attention to your spelling and grammar. Mistakes in this area can make reading even a one-page document extremely difficult and frustrating, resulting in your ideas not being taken seriously.

The goal is for your documents to showcase your ideas, not show a sloppy and lackluster attention to detail. To assist you in this area, consider the following suggestions:

- Apply everything you learned from elementary school through high school and college.
- Purchase a book on basic grammar and apply it.

- You cannot survive in the business community merely on bullet points and sentence fragments.

- Always proofread your document at least once for spelling and grammar.

- Ask coworkers to proofread your documents— fresh eyes always help.

Recipients. Determining who should receive your documents can be difficult. You want to ensure that the proper individuals receive a copy of your work, but you do not want to clutter the desks of fellow employees unnecessarily. With more experience you will be able to more quickly and effectively determine who should and who should not receive your documents. But, for right now, ask your mentor, coworkers, and boss who should receive your work.

Segmentation. Segmenting your memo into specific sections is important because you want to give your audience the ability to quickly identify the purpose of your memo and the conclusions you have reached. The suggested template contains four distinct sections—issue, proposal, analysis, and conclusion. It is important to incorporate all of these sections in the specific order to ensure that your information is conveyed in the proper manner:

- Issue—This section should not be more than three sentences. If you cannot articulate the issue in three sentences then you have not completely formulated the problem; remember, whoever you are presenting the issue to does not have the time to read a dissertation on the problem.

- Proposal—This section should also be no more than three sentences. You need to be able to describe your resolution clearly, concisely, and quickly. Moreover, there is nothing wrong with stating in this section that a project needs to be opened to investigate possible resolutions. By providing such a proposal, you are informing your audience that you are requesting approval to spend time on determining a possible solution.

- Analysis—This section does not have a length limitation; however, it is always important to be concise and organized. This is the section that articulates how you determined there was a problem and how you determined the resolution you are suggesting. Be sure to cite specifics not generalizations.

- Conclusion—This is a reiteration of your proposal. It is important to restate your proposal at the end because you want all readers to end their reading of your document with your proposal clearly in their mind.

Length. In most instances your memo should be no longer than one page. I know this may seem like an impossible task at times but it is important to remember that the longer it takes for you to convey your message, the higher the possibility of creating confusion and losing the attention of your audience. Your audience members are busy people who do not have the time to sift through your analysis—it is your job to sift through the analysis and devise a solution.

Retention. You should keep a paper or electronic copy of all documentation so that you can reference it later. Having these documents on hand can be very helpful when seeking promotions, using them as an example for future projects, and for many other purposes.

> *Anytime you bring a problem to your boss or coworker make sure that you have a solid suggestion on how to fix it.*

A good example of a corporate memo incorporating these principles is shown on page 34. Having the document creation date and any update dates allows readers of the memo to validate that they have the right version of the document. By having the document creator's name on the document along with the recipients, all readers have information about who is involved in the memo's decision points. Dividing the memo into specific logical segments (Issue, Proposal, Analysis—Reasons for Stopping the Project, Conclusion) allows for (1) quick analysis by the readers, (2) easy reference back to the memo, and (3) readers can skip to segments

Corporate Memo—Good

Page 1 of 1

Date: 01/01/10
Update: 01/22/10
Department: Information Technology

Creator: Adam Scholl, Business Analyst, Development Team
Recipients: John Stove, Project Manager
                         Sophia Counter, Business Analyst
                         Elizabeth Floore, Programmer
Project Number: 0123245
Project Name: Making employee personal information updates
                              automatic

Issue
The project is four months behind schedule and over
budget by $80,000.

Proposal
Put the project on hold.

Reasons for stopping the project
The project should be stopped for the following
reasons: ....

Conclusion
It is recommended that the project be stopped
because...

that they are most interested in. The document has an overall professionalism that gives it authority.

Now review the poor memo example on this page. You can see immediately that the format of the memo takes away from the message that is trying to be conveyed. Different font sizes and styles makes it harder for the reader to focus on the content. Equally important, by not having headings in the memo, the reader has to read the entire memo instead of being able to skip to the sections that are of particular interest.

CORPORATE MEMO—POOR

01/01/10

Developer-Steve Johnson

Audience-IT Team

Making employee personal updates automatice-0123245

The purpose of this memo is to introduce a new project and the reasons why the project is being created. The project will provide better service and functionality to our clients...

Comparing the good memo example with the bad memo example clearly illustrates the importance of creating a professional document.

E-MAIL

E-mail has become an important form of communication in the business environment. Somehow, it has also become an abyss where it is (erroneously) perceived as acceptable to act as though you are not at work. This abyss does not exist, no matter what you may believe or what you may perceive from others. Some people foolishly believe that because they are using e-mail, basic professionalism does not apply, and they write e-mails as though they are talking to a friend or to an enemy. E-mails sent at work must always be professional. When in doubt, equate your e-mail to giving a presentation to the board of directors. Follow these core principles at all times:

- Write your e-mails as though you are writing a memo or talking to a coworker.
- Always be professional when writing an e-mail.
- Keep your e-mail short and concise.
- Always review your e-mails for spelling and grammar errors prior to sending them.

PERSONAL ACCOUNT

I once sent an e-mail that I hastily put together on Friday evening before leaving for the weekend. I remember thinking when I was writing the e-mail that I was breaking my core e-mail principles but I let it slide because it was a Friday and I was in a hurry; I assumed everyone would understand. However, when I arrived at work on Monday the e-mail that I sent out on Friday had caused a chain reaction of e-mails during the weekend (yes, people do review their e-mails during the weekend). Because it was so poorly written, my team spent hours working on the wrong issue during the weekend. I had to bring the team together and apologize for my mistake. This was the last time I broke my own rules and the last time I sent out a quick e-mail on a Friday evening without thoroughly reviewing it.

Do not write e-mails in haste. If an e-mail must be sent, take the appropriate time to send out a professional document.

The principles that follow should be applied when you are writing any e-mail at work.

Recipients. When sending an e-mail, it is important to know what priority status your e-mail should have and exactly who should receive it:

- **To**—Adding a person's name to the recipient list means you want that person to read your e-mail and be part of the communication channel that you opened.

  **To: John Force, George Mason,
         Jennifer Maxwell, Beth Williamson**

Make sure that you only include persons that you want and are expecting to read and possibly respond to your e-mail.

- **Cc**—Adding a person's name to this section means that you are just giving them a heads up. In other words, it signifies that you do not expect them to respond to the e-mail.

  **To: John Force, George Mason, Jennifer
         Maxwell, Beth Williamson**
  Cc: Steve Forester, John Gonzalez

Do not include everyone on the team in this section. If you are discussing a problem with one or two coworkers, then just communicate with those individuals. Do not copy every person while you have a limited communication channel open.

- **Bcc**—Adding a person's name to this section means that you want that person, more likely than not a boss/mentor, to be aware of the correspondence, but you do not want those receiving the e-mail to be aware that you sent it to this person.

To : **John Force, George Mason, Jennifer Maxwell, Beth Williamson**

Cc : **Steve Forester, John Gonzale**

Bcc :Jim Jones

Do not include anyone in this section if you really want them to read the e-mail; they probably will not read it. Instead, resend the e-mail to your boss/mentor using the To section and inform him/her that you are sending the e-mail as a heads up. This will ensure the e-mail is given the necessary attention.

Subject. The subject heading of an e-mail is very important but is often underutilized. Given the prevalence of e-mail as a communication tool, e-mail inboxes can easily become flooded with dozens of messages. Some are important, some are not. Therefore, properly titling your e-mail messages will ensure that your intended recipients recognize the importance of the e-mail you are sending.

Follow these basic guidelines for the title to ensure that your e-mail is given the appropriate attention by your recipients:

- Make the title short and concise.
- When appropriate, include the project name or the issue in the title.
- Proper grammar and spelling is always appropriate. Here is a sample:

To: **John Force, George Mason, Jennifer Maxwell, Beth Williamson**

Cc: **Steve Forester, John Gonzalez**

Bcc: **Jim Jones**

Subject: **Project # 12346: Installing .NET Framework—Status of the Project**

The information in the subject line has been segmented into three sections: project number, project name, and the reason for the e-mail. This allows the receiver to quickly determine the importance of the e-mail and to handle it accordingly.

> *You can change the subject line of e-mails that have been sent to you by highlighting it and typing over it. This will allow you to categorize your e-mails according to your personal order.*

Format. As I have already mentioned in the section on memos, the format and presentation of your e-mail message is just as important as the content of the message itself. Use the following guidelines:

- Use Times New Roman, size 10 or 12 as your font.

- Do not use colors in your e-mail.

- Remember, your e-mail can and will be forwarded to others!

- Use headings and subheadings when necessary.

Spelling and Grammar. You must use proper spelling and grammar at all times. Write as though you are writing a memo to your boss. Review your e-mails prior to sending them to ensure that your spelling and grammar are correct.

Tone. It is easy for a reader of an e-mail to take the wrong message from it because of the tone. So it is important that you read over your e-mail prior to sending it to ensure that it does not come across as rude or disrespectful.

Length. Because e-mail is a quick form of communication, your e-mail should not be more than four paragraphs in length. If your message requires more than a few full paragraphs, then do not use e-mail; create a memo or reorganize your thoughts to make the e-mail shorter.

People have a tendency not to read long e-mail messages in full. In addition, long e-mails are not given the same authority as memos.

Auto Signature. While an auto signature is a handy tool, people often include too much information in it. Your auto signature is used to inform recipients who you are. Only put your name, title, e-mail, phone number, extension number, and location in your auto signature:

. . . .

Adam Scholl
Business Analyst
Development Team, IT
adamscholl@corporation.com
800 555 1234 ext. 1145

Do not include quotations, clip art, unusual fonts, or other miscellaneous information in your auto signature. The extra information could be offensive to others and it is not professional.

Message Content. The content of your e-mail message will be reflective of the purpose of the e-mail. Here are the two most common types of e-mail messages along with suggestions to assist you in determining what types of information to include:

- **Type 1: E-mail that asks questions of the team**—Structure such e-mails by first indicating in the subject line that you are asking a question of the team. Then reiterate in the first sentence the question(s) you are asking followed by a sentence thanking the intended recipients for their time and attention in the matter. Always include a time frame for when you need their answers so that your recipients can plan their work schedule accordingly. Your questions should be complete sentences. Conclude by thanking your recipient for help in answering your questions.

- **Type 2: E-mail to disseminate information**— Include in the subject line or title the type of information you are trying disseminate; for instance, is it a status e-mail or a notification that you will be out of the office? Reiterate in the first sentence what you trying to inform your audience of. If the email is communicating a direction to be taken, then indicate the issue, your analysis, and your conclusion in separate paragraph(s). Be concise; remember it is an e-mail. Thank anyone who helped in reaching the conclusion. It is important to give credit where credit is due. Conclude by indicating how you want questions, concerns, or comments to be addressed to you and the e-mail group. For instance, you may say "Please forward any comments, questions, or concerns to me."

What Not to Include. In addition to knowing the essential information to include in an e-mail, it is also important to understand what you must not include in an e-mail. The following list is intended to ensure you do not get into trouble in this area. Following this list will get you into a professional habit that you will use your entire career:

- Never send e-mails that contain jokes: No exceptions to this rule!
- Do not use inappropriate language in e-mails.
- Do not flirt or make sexual advances in e-mails.
- Do not use your business e-mail to send or receive personal messages.
- Do not give your work e-mail to friends or family; they could accidentally send a virus to your corporate e-mail.

- Never respond to or forward inappropriate e-mails.

- If someone at your work continually sends you inappropriate e-mails, ask him/her to stop in person.

- Never open attachments from someone you don't know; moreover, scan any attachments that seem suspicious.

- Scan *all* attachments for viruses.

PERSONAL ACCOUNT

An e-mail reportedly was sent by a high-level executive containing an attachment. I was suspicious of the e-mail because the body of the e-mail was written in an unprofessional manner. Hence I chose to delete the e-mail without opening the attachment. However, a few members within the IT department did open the attachment resulting in a virus infiltrating the company's network because the e-mail was bogus. The persons who opened the e-mail were formally reprimanded because they had not been careful enough in screening their incoming e-mails.

Here is an example of an e-mail incorporating the suggested principles.

E-MAIL—GOOD

To: **John Force, George Mason, Jennifer Maxwell, Beth Williamson**

Cc: **Steve Forester, John Gonzalez**

Subject: **12346 Installing VB Framework— Installation Status**

John, George, Jennifer, and Beth,

This email offers status on the installation of VB Framework on the first two developer's computers.

The installation of the VB Framework on Steve's and John's development workstations didn't succeed. At this time we don't know why the installation failed. Furthermore, because the failure caused unexpected failures of other applications on their workstations we uninstalled all of the successful packages.

We are currently investigating why the installation failed and will update everyone at the close of business tomorrow.

Please, contact me by e-mail if you have any questions, comments, or concerns.

Thank you,

Adam Scholl
Business Analyst
Development Team, IT
adamscholl@corporation.com
800 555 1234 ext. 1145

Note that the subject line specifically states what project the e-mail pertains to and the reason for the e-mail (the status of the project). This allows for quick review and organization. Second, the To line indicates the specific people who are being asked to review the e-mail. The body of the e-mail reiterates the purpose in the first sentence and then provides a quick overview of the purpose of the email—to provide a status of the project. Fourth, the closing of the e-mail is a short-concise statement.

Here is an example of an e-mail that does not incorporate the suggested principles.

E-Mail—Poor

To:	**John Force, George Mason, Jennifer Maxwell, Beth Williamson**
Cc:	**Steve Forester, John Gonzalez**
Subject:	**Status**

Everyone,

This e-mail is inteended to tell status of project—it is going well I will send status again next week

Contact me if you need anything

Thank you,

Adam Scholl
'A-Team'

Reviewing the poor example, notice the incorrect spelling and the incorrect grammar. These simple mistakes take away from the purpose of the e-mail. Furthermore, directing the e-mail to "everyone" implies that the message is intended for the persons that are cc'd. Equally important, the subject line states only "status," which is not specific enough. Telling your audience to contact you if they need anything may result in persons contacting you for help in matters that have nothing to do with your communication, Finally, what does "A-Team" have to do with anything in the e-mail?

PHONE ETIQUETTE

The ability to speak effectively on the phone is absolutely crucial in the workplace. You have to remember that when you are speaking on the phone, the person on the other end cannot see you. While this seems obvious, the consequences of that lack of visual presence are not as obvious.

People who are unable to see you talking may be more likely to make quick judgments based on your voice, articulation, mannerisms, and so on. These judgments could put you at a disadvantage regarding your future interaction with those individuals. This, in turn, puts you at a disadvantage with the entity those individuals represent. It is important to be courteous and professional at all times.

The following principles can be applied to help ensure your phone conversations are always conducted in a professional manner.

Answer the Phone Professionally. While it may seem like common sense, this simple action is often underemphasized or ignored. While you can answer the phone in a variety of ways, you want to make sure you introduce yourself in a courteous manner. For example, answer the phone by saying, "This is Adam in the Accounting Department, how may I help you?"

Remember, you want to be a leader, not a follower. Do not follow the lead of a person who answers the phone in an unprofessional manner.

Give the Conversation Your Full Attention. If there is one thing that can drive a caller crazy, it is the realization that the person on the other end of the line is not taking his or her call seriously. This is easier to pick up on than you think so you have to be careful.

Here are a few tips that you can follow to avoid aggravating clients and coworkers:

- Do not conduct other work or talk to others when answering the phone.
- If conducting a meeting in your cubicle, excuse yourself prior to answering the call.
- If it is not an emergency, explain to the caller that you are in a meeting.
- Give the caller a time when you will call them back.

> *The above rules apply when using an office phone, cell phone, home phone, and so on.*

- Always keep pen and paper within easy reach of the phone. This avoids frantic searches for these materials when you need them and enables you to jot down pertinent information during the conversation.

Use Proper English. It is imperative that you use proper English when at work, even if you are talking to friends or family. Although using proper English on the phone may not seem that important, it ensures that you do not become accustomed to using improper language in the workplace. In addition, it ensures that you are not overheard using inappropriate language by a coworker, superior, or—worse yet—a customer!

End the Conversation Professionally. Above all else, you want to maintain your professional etiquette throughout the entire conversation. Thus, be sure to end the conversation in a courteous and professional manner. Keep in mind that this entails more than just thanking the person for their time.

The checklist that follows will help you make sure you have covered all your bases prior to ending a call:

- Make sure you have answered all of the caller's questions.

- Ensure that all of your own questions have been answered.
- Write down all necessary follow-up questions and actions.
- End with an appropriate closing.
- If the conversation warrants a follow-up e-mail or memo, do it immediately!

Following Up on a Call. While you may initially find it difficult to assess the need for follow-up communication, your skills in this area will improve over time. For now, perform a follow-up communication in the following circumstances:

- When the conversation was long and cumbersome (ensures all parties understand and have an accurate record of what took place),
- When either party required further actions items, or
- When you believe that the subject matter deserves a follow up.

Voice-Mail Settings. It is important to make sure that your voice-mail settings are professional. Spend the necessary time to ensure they clearly indicate who you are, your department, and your extension.

What Not to Do. While it is important that you are aware of many of the fundamentals of phone etiquette, it is equally important that you recognize actions that should be avoided at all costs. For example, do not put someone on hold to vent your frustration. Do not place someone on hold to speak negatively of him/her. There is a real possibility that you can fail to actually place them on hold or that someone can hear what you are saying.

PERSONAL ACCOUNT

We were on a conference call with two vendors that became very intense. The conversation resulted in all organizations placing the blame on each other for not meeting particular deadlines. I informed all parties on the phone that we were going to place them on hold while we discussed some matters in private. My real intention was for all parties to have a moment to relax and refocus on the matter at hand. However, one vendor believed that when we put him on hold we could not hear him. After listening to a few unpleasant words about me, I abruptly took the phone off hold and explained we had heard what he said. I ended the meeting—to ensure that I did not become unprofessional—and asked the manager of the offending vendor to call me. Subsequently, the relationship between our companies quickly deteriorated to the point that they lost our future business.

Vendor

In the information technology industry, a vendor represents a company that is supplying a product to another company.

Do *not* answer the phone if you cannot afford the time to help someone. If you are on your way to a meeting or are leaving for the day and your phone rings, do not answer it because you will only frustrate yourself and the person trying to get in touch with you. If the phone call is an emergency, the individual calling will reach you by a different manner.

> *Always inform someone, either by phone or e-mail, when you will respond to them. This showcases your professionalism. More importantly, it allows the other person to schedule his/her day appropriately and it demonstrates your thoughtful consideration and respect for that person.*

Do *not* speak so loudly that everyone else in the office can hear. This point needs little clarification. When you are speaking on the phone, ensure that you do so in a manner that does not disturb those around you.

Never lose your temper while speaking to anyone on the phone. If you believe that you are going to lose your cool then excuse yourself from the call. Moreover, do not return the phone call until you have relaxed.

Being unprofessional on the phone is no better than being unprofessional in person.

> Create a sign to place by your phone that states:
> **Be Professional on the Phone.**
> This will help remind you that even during difficult phone calls you should be professional.

BUSINESS PRESENTATIONS

Presentations will be an important part of your career because they are opportunities for you to show others your professionalism in a unique setting. When you make a presentation, you are at that moment an expert on the subject that you are talking about; moreover, you have the attention of an audience that is looking to you for direction. It is important for you to take your presentations seriously.

When you are first informed that you have to make a presentation, you need to plan accordingly. To do this, you need to first determine what type of presentation this will be: discussion or educational. A discussion presentation is less formal and is intended for you to be more of a moderator. An educational presentation will require you to be the educator on a given subject matter. This will require you to be a subject matter expert and usually requires more time. We'll spend a little time discussing each of these presentation types.

Discussion Presentation

As the moderator of a discussion presentation, you will be required to facilitate the meeting. This means moving the discussion presentation along toward a particular predefined goal. You will need to thoroughly understand the desired goal of the discussion before you attempt to facilitate it. (Please review Chapter 3, "Essentials of Being a Facilitator.")

Equally important, you will need to have an understanding of the subject matter that you will be presenting. This means that you do not have to be the subject matter expert, but you need to ensure that you have enough knowledge to be able to facilitate the discussion.

Subject Matter Expert—SME

A person who is designated as an expert in a particular matter.

In a discussion presentation, the atmosphere is usually informal; however, that does not mean your presentation will be less professional. To ensure that your presentation is professional use the following guidelines:

1. Make an outline of what you will be discussing; this is separate from a meeting agenda. (Creating

a meeting agenda is discussed in Chapter 3, "Essentials of Being a Facilitator.")

2. From this outline, determine the key subjects that will be discussed. These key subjects will be the points you make sure the group addresses.

3. Determine the length of the meeting.

4. If the meeting is less than thirty minutes, use handouts that have the key points listed as a presentation aid.

5. Ensure that your handout is short and concise but that it also specifies all of the key points.

6. You can use more than one page for discussion meetings that are over thirty minutes.

7. Using PowerPoint slides for a discussion meeting is not recommended unless you are a subject matter expert. Using PowerPoint won't allow the attendees to take the information back with them, unless you also print handouts, and there may be too much information for the audience to digest. A handout gives the attendees time to digest the information in a manner that allows them to ask and get answers to critical questions.

Notice that the example handout specifies the date, project name, and the matter being discussed. This allows the receiver of the handout to refer to the handout in the future and to catalog the handout accordingly. Furthermore, the handout has specific headings that

Handout

Discussion Topic: Action Figure Product Placement Failure
Date: 2/10/10
Project: 62347—Action Figure
Created: Adam Scholl
Issue: Action figure is not selling as expected
Product: Action Figure

Characteristics

. . . .

Demographics of Product

. . .

Product Pre-Assessment

Purchasing Party Demographics

. . .

Cost of Good

. . . .

Price

. . . . . .

Suspected Reasons for Failure

Price
Data has shown that the product price is . . .

. . . .

provide a natural flow during your discussion and specific points to reference. Moreover, add any information that you believe needs to be discussed in greater depth. Last, even though it is a handout, it should be professionally written to ensure that your status as a professional is recognized.

> *You may have unexpected attendees so print one extra handout for every five people. This will ensure that drop-ins get the information.*

Educational Presentation

An educational presentation is intended to teach others about a subject matter. This type of presentation requires you not only to be the facilitator but also to be the subject matter expert on the subject being presented. (Please review Chapter 3, "Essentials of Being a Facilitator.") You will need to answer questions and/or direct people to additional resources as necessary to handle all aspects of the topic.

PowerPoint is useful for this type of presentation because the attendees expect to get a lot of information in a short time.

The following guidelines will allow you to create a professional educational presentation using PowerPoint:

1. Create an outline of the educational presentation.

2. Add any specific information into your outline that will allow you to answer questions that may be difficult; moreover, add any information that will allow you to bring up an important educational point.

3. Take the key points from your outline and add them to your PowerPoint slide. Do not overwhelm the PowerPoint slide with information. A PowerPoint presentation is an outline of your discussion so treat it as such.

4. Ensure that you have a back-up plan if your PowerPoint presentation does not work. (More about this in Chapter 3, "Essentials of Being a Facilitator.")

Educational Presentation Examples

Note: The following examples were taken from an educational presentation that I gave to my French Law class while attending University of Detroit Mercy School of Law. I choose to use this as an example because by following my own rules I developed a good presentation after I had failed when I did not follow the rules. And, Yes, law schools have classes such as French Law. And, No, it was not as easy as I had hoped it would have been.

First Slide—Intro to Topic

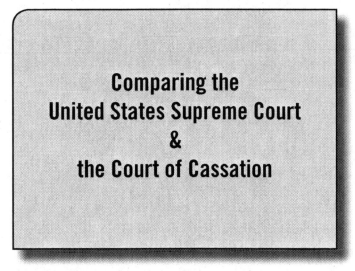

The first slide informs the audience of the subject that will be taught. The first slide is the point where you give any necessary introductions and so on.

Second Slide—Agenda

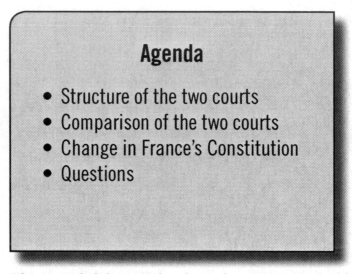

Agenda

- Structure of the two courts
- Comparison of the two courts
- Change in France's Constitution
- Questions

The second slide provides the audience an agenda of what will be discussed. This allows audience members to prepare mentally and you to set the ground rules of what will be discussed and when. If the meeting is longer than one hour, then it would be beneficial to add the time each subject will be discussed and for how long. This will ensure that time schedules are met and your audience members will be prepared if you have to move quickly at times to keep up with the designated times.

Third Slide—Educational Portion

The third slide is an example of how a teaching slide should be structured. These slides should not be filled with a lot of information because it will overwhelm the viewers. If a smaller font has to be used to fit in all the information the viewer will have a hard time reading the slide. Moreover, your audience will spend more time reading the slides instead of listening to you. I did add a quote in this slide because I needed to refer to its specific language during my discussion. Also, the second bullet point, The Judiciary Act of 1789, is included in the slide because there is a direct relationship between it and the first bullet point. If there was no relationship then I would have put the second bullet point in its own slide. It is important to structure your slides in a logical manner that will not confuse your audience.

Fourth Slide—Ending

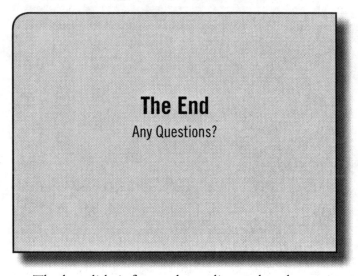

The last slide informs the audience that the presentation is over and allows for time to answer questions. If you provide your audience time to ask questions, you need to be prepared to answer the questions.

The next slide is a bad example, which was part of my educational presentation.

Slide—Poor

Comparison: Judicial Review

- **France**
  - France has been averse to judicial review of legislation. Since the Revolution of 1789, a strict separation of powers rule prevailed and the judiciary was not given the right ti interfere with the activities of the legislature. While during the Ancient Regime judges could contest the legitimacy of a bill passed by the legislative power, "no court since the Revolution has ever invalidated or otherwise refused to apply a statute on the grounds that it was unconstitutional."

- **America**
  - Thus, contrary to what happened in the United States (where the Supreme Court, "with a stroke of genius," acknowledged its power to review legislation, making true Madison's motto that "ambition must be made to counteract ambition")

[1] Supremacy of Parliament and the lack of judicial review have been the defining features of French "Jacobian constitutionalism" since the time of the Revolution"

This is a poor slide for numerous reasons. First, there is way too much information. It is hard to see and read. Moreover, in my presentation, this slide was probably a distraction because it is hard to read. Second, having this much information turns the slide into a crutch, which will cause you to become disconnected from your audience. I added a footnote which is a great practice because you can refer your audience to this information if they want to do further research; however, the footnote is too small for it to be any help.

Next is the same PowerPoint slide after I incorporated my own rules.

Slide—Better

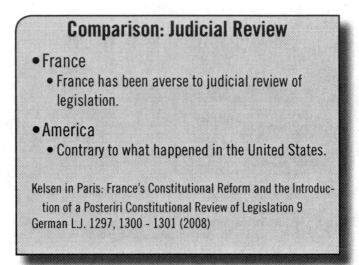

This version of the slide is better for numerous reasons. First, there is less information so it is readable and not distracting. This version would have allowed me to maintain my audience's attention. The citation information is also readable so individuals can review the information on their own if they want to. I removed the third bullet point because after reviewing the slide I realized that there was no direct relationship between the two previous bullet points. Removing the third bullet point allowed for a more cohesive discussion. This slide looks more polished and professional which gives automatic authority.

IN CONCLUSION

There was a lot of information in this chapter—how to create a professional memo and e-mail, proper phone etiquette, and creating a professional business presentation. Each section provided specifics on how to be a professional in your work. The overarching theme is creating professionalism in everything you do. Consistently presenting and creating professional work will increase your stature in your company.

CHAPTER 3

MEETINGS

The most important thing for a young man is to establish a credit . . . a reputation, character.

—JOHN D. ROCKEFELLER

CHAPTER CONCEPTS

The Importance of Meetings

Essential Factors for a
Successful Meeting

Corporate Conveyance Meetings

Decision-Making Meetings

Essentials of Being a Facilitator

THE IMPORTANCE OF MEETINGS

Meetings are commonly held when people need to communicate with one another. For instance, parents meet with teachers to understand the academic progress of their children. People meet with members of the police department to learn what to do to combat crime in their neighborhoods. In each of these situations, the meeting serves a distinct purpose, but success is dependent on many factors. This is why a chapter has been devoted to the concept of meetings.

ESSENTIAL FACTORS FOR A SUCCESSFUL MEETING

Business meetings are no different than other meetings; they require some essential factors in order to be successful. For a business meeting to be successful, and for you to be a part of that success, it is essential that you understand your role in the meeting. Start by familiarizing yourself with the two most frequent reasons for having a meeting:

1. To allow an organization to convey information to its employees, and
2. To facilitate employee decision making.

If the predominant reason for holding a meeting is to allow an organization such as a corporation to convey information to its employees, the meeting is known as a corporate conveyance meeting and is integral to the corporate atmosphere. Corporations use conveyance meetings to inform employees of corporate goals, benefits, human resources policies, and so on. These meetings serve as valuable venues to disseminate vital corporate information. More often than not, these meetings are conducted by the human resource department and/or upper management.

> *The role of the attendee in this type of meeting is to listen and learn.*

The second reason for holding a meeting is to give employees an opportunity to work together in making decisions. The ability to make decisions is a complex process that, at a minimum, requires employees to first collect the necessary data to make an informed decision. This information can be collected using a variety of different methods, such as *bing* (Microsoft's version of google), e-mail, books, and decision-making meetings. Decision-making meetings are often structured around the decision-making methodology of the facilitator(s), that is, they are reflective of the decision-making style of those conducting the meeting. So it is important to be open to the different methods and styles that you may encounter.

Your role in this type of meeting will be based on the facilitator's decision-making methodology; the structure of your team; the corporate structure; and the skills, knowledge, and expertise that you personally bring to the discussion. You will need to be flexible when it comes to what is demanded of a specific role from a specific facilitator.

As you grow in your professional career, so will your understanding of the complexities of the business meetings conducted at your company. By building on this framework, you will become an effective professional. The next sections describe in greater detail how you should conduct yourself in these types of meetings and also what types of behaviors to avoid.

> *Remember, a decision-making meeting is dynamic, so you must remain flexible.*

CORPORATE CONVEYANCE MEETINGS

As an attendee at a corporate conveyance meeting, your role is to listen and learn. It is not your job to inform others of what you know. In other words, these meetings are for you to educate yourself about the corporation and its policies. Therefore, take these meetings seriously.

Attendance Is a MUST. Unless otherwise instructed by your manager or mentor, attend *all* corporate conveyance meetings. Do not skip a meeting just because some of your coworkers have decided not to attend. Do not be a follower when your career depends on it!

Bring All Necessary Materials. The golden rule for attending any meeting is that you should always be prepared. Regardless of the role you assume in a meeting, you want to bring the following essential materials:

- Pen and paper,
- Any pertinent information that was passed out prior to the meeting,
- A folder to organize your materials, and
- Your business cards.

If you do not bring these simple materials with you, it gives the impression that you are not interested in the meeting. Needless to say, boredom or disinterest is certainly not a sentiment you wish to portray to others—especially your bosses.

Arrive Early. Although you will frequently be pressed for time as you begin your corporate career, arriving early is important for two simple reasons:

1. It ensures that you have a place to sit, and

2. Punctuality demonstrates reliability.

A corporate conveyance meeting is the perfect opportunity to network with bosses and coworkers. This is an important function of your career—so do not underestimate its importance! Network, network, network!!! Take the time to introduce yourself to anyone you do not know. Try to make it a habit to introduce yourself to at least two people per meeting.

Notify Others of Your Attendance. Despite all evidence to the contrary, your bosses and coworkers cannot keep track of where you are and what you are doing at all times. Thus, it is a good idea to let others know that you will be attending the meeting. This will avoid any misunderstanding regarding your whereabouts. In addition, also remember to abide by the following tips:

- Mark the meeting in your electronic calendar.

- Factor in the necessary travel time to and from the meeting.

- Put a sign in your cube stating that you are at a meeting and where that meeting is being held (also a good idea when you go to lunch).

- Turn off all electronic gadgets. Be sure to double and triple check that all of your electronic gadgets are off. It is rude and unprofessional to have electronic equipment ring during a meeting. You will know when you are in the position to keep them on, but trust me, you are not there yet!

PERSONAL ACCOUNT

I was attending a corporate conveyance meeting in which a vice-president was the facilitator. The vice-president had been speaking for about ten minutes when a cell phone rang which caused a moment of disturbance. Now, at this point I re-checked my phone to ensure it was off, which most attendees did; however, within a few moments another person's cell phone rang. This time the ring tone was pretty disruptive. As you can imagine, there was a quick burst of laughter but then the laughter turned into embarrassment for the person who had left his phone on. This was a less-than-funny moment that reflected a real lapse in professionalism.

Prepare for the Meeting. Like everything else in life, preparation is essential to success. By taking the time to prepare, even for meetings where you have a minor role, you will become more confident and comfortable in your position. Here are a few things you can do to prepare for the meeting:

- Read all pertinent information prior to the meeting.
- Use the bathroom facilities prior to the meeting.
- Do not smoke for at least thirty minutes before a meeting and if you are a smoker be sure to carry breath mints. Stay away from onions and garlic

as well, no one wants to talk to someone with offensive breath.

Listen and Learn. Take down notes, questions, and your thoughts. This will allow you to grow as an employee. Remember, this is your career, not just a job.

Do Not Ask Questions at Inappropriate Times. Nothing can be more disruptive than an inappropriate and ill-timed question. Not only can you break up the momentum of the meeting, but you can also aggravate other attendees. To help ensure the meeting is smooth and productive, keep the following points in mind when asking questions during a meeting:

- Questions should be asked at the end of the meeting or during a designated period.

- Be sure your questions cannot be answered by re-reading the provided material.

- Consider whether your questions could better be answered by your mentor or through an e-mail to the meeting facilitator(s). For example, does your question pertain to a matter that is of little interest or concern to the other meeting participants? If the answer is yes, the question should not take up time at the meeting.

- Do not extend the meeting time by asking questions that can be easily answered using other forms of communication.

Do Not Arrive Late! There is absolutely no reason you should arrive late to a meeting. Not only are individuals who arrive late disrespectful of other attendees, but they also miss out on important networking opportunities and collaborative discussions that can occur prior to the meeting. Moreover, you are not in the position in your career where you can miss such corporate meetings. These types of meetings are developed specifically for you.

Do Not Leave Early. The only time it is acceptable to leave a meeting early is during an absolute emergency, such as sickness. Realistically, the chances that a work-related emergency will require your immediate attention are slim to none. Remember, at the early stage of your career, you still lack any pertinent and critical knowledge that only you can provide to your coworkers. However, if you know in advance that you will need to leave early, make sure you remember to do the following:

- Notify the facilitator prior to the meeting.
- Take a seat close to the exit to avoid interrupting others when you leave.

Personal Account

I started my career going to meetings without understanding and appreciating their importance; I grew to understand how meetings can waste resources within an organization. I once worked with a high-level executive who had an unwritten rule that if you were late to a meeting he did not want you to come to the meeting. He did not tolerate the interruption but he also wanted to re-enforce his belief that meetings needed to be taken seriously. One day an attendee showed up late for a meeting and the discussion stopped. The person apologized for being late. This facilitator stopped the meeting and told the person to leave because if he was late for an issue that was more important than this meeting then he needed to attend to it. If the issue was not that important, then he should not have come late and caused the meeting to lose momentum. Whether or not you agree with this facilitator's style, it is important to show respect by showing up on time.

Do Not Have Side Conversations. It is rude, not to mention extremely unprofessional, to have side conversations during a meeting. When you begin conducting meetings of your own, you will quickly recognize that a side conversation can be very distracting.

Do Not Act Like You Don't Care. This ranks right up there with arriving late to a meeting on the nonprofessional scale. Although you may think you appear attentive, there are several nonverbal cues that you need to avoid. Make sure that you do not fall asleep. Believe it or not, employees do this frequently, and head-bobbing and drooling are never positive behavior at the office.

If you begin to feel sleepy, start writing every other sentence the facilitator says on your pad of paper. Do not doodle and do not jiggle, both will be noticed.

Side conversations should not occur; not even to keep you alert. Give your full attention to the facilitator. Be sure to sit up straight during the entire meeting—posture is important to keeping you looking alert and interested.

DECISION-MAKING MEETINGS

As an attendee at a decision-making meeting, your role will depend on the type of decision being made. While your participation in this type of meeting will be more active, there are still pertinent do's and don'ts. Regardless of your role at this type of meeting, you are still an attendee, and you must act accordingly.

Know Your Role. If you are unsure of your role in the meeting, then ask your mentor, boss, or coworker. You could also simply ask the person(s) who set up the meeting. Do not go to a meeting without knowing what contributions will be required from you.

Prepare. As mentioned several times already, preparation is a key component for anything and everything you do in the corporate world (and in life in general). If you will be contributing information that has been requested, make sure that you prepare appropriately. Do not come to the meeting without having some suggestions to resolve the problem being discussed. If you do not have the answers, then you need to explain what you have done up to that point and have some idea how much longer it will take you to come up with an answer. In addition, remember the following:

- Read all information that has been sent out regarding the purpose of the meeting.

- Bring all documentation that has been provided regarding the purpose of the meeting.

- Bring any information that will back up your answers to any questions.

- Be sure to organize your thoughts and research prior to the meeting.

- Write down any questions that you have for individuals who will be attending the meeting.

- Do not blindside someone during a meeting.

Blindsiding

This is when someone intentionally fails to inform someone else of information in order to make that person look bad in front of others.

Wear Proper Attire. I addressed the subject of proper attire in Chapter 1 so I will not delve into it too deeply here. However, I do want to mention a few specific points that focus on professional attire in a meeting setting:

- Be conscious of your attire when attending a meeting.

- If meeting with clients, customers, vendors, or potential employees, dress according to company standards.

- Do not smoke or eat onions or garlic for at least thirty minutes before the meeting. If you are a smoker, carry breath mints. You will be in close proximity to other people and your breath needs to be inoffensive.

Arrive at Least Five Minutes Before It Starts. This will allow you ample time to compose yourself, make introductions, and finalize any last-minute preparations.

Introduce Yourself to Attendees that You Do Not Know. Acknowledge those whom you have met before. Remember, meetings are great opportunities to network and showcase your professionalism.

Network, Network, Network!

Take an Active Role in the Meeting. Your presence at the meeting did not occur by chance. You were invited to be a part of the meeting for a reason, so assume an active role.

Listen and Think before You Speak. This should be obvious, but I have seen people fail to do it more and more in recent years. Despite what you might think and despite what you have heard, speed does not equal accuracy. If the difference between a quick wrong answer and a slow correct answer is thirty seconds, those around you will be happy to wait. Trust me on this one:

- Listen to what is being said before you speak. Do not formulate your answer while someone is speaking.

- Answer the question being asked. Do not guess or give a run-around answer. If you do not know the answer, say so, your candor will be appreciated.

Take Proper Notes. Good information to annotate may include the names of those who attended, the subject matter discussed, projects assigned, conclusions reached, and so on.

Do Not Arrive Late. I know I said it before but it bears repeating. If you arrive late, do not cause a disruption when entering the meeting. Pick the closest available seat. Do not greet friends and coworkers or do anything that draws more attention to your late arrival. Be as unobtrusive as possible. Do not open your laptop, briefcase, can of soda, or anything else after the meeting has started. Take what you need out of your briefcase before entering the meeting.

> *Review your notes after the meeting to ensure you recognize any necessary follow-up work.*

Do Not Leave Early. If you must leave early due to a work-related conflict, inform the facilitator prior to the meeting. You can do this in person or through e-mail.

Do Not Speak Out of Turn. Make sure that you speak only when it is appropriate. Do not interrupt other people. If you do not know the answer, then say so. Remember, time is precious, but so is accurate and reliable information. If you do not know the answer to a question, provide a time frame when you will have the answer. Remember to give yourself enough time to find the answer. Be sure to write down the question. Get the answer to the person you committed to by the date/time you specified.

Your reputation is on the line, so if you state you will have an answer by a certain date/time, you must follow through with that promise.

PERSONAL ACCOUNT

I was the leader of a project that required face time with a vendor. The vendor came on site for a week for discussions on the needs of the product. A new associate raised his hand to indicate that he had to leave the meeting early, which shocked me. I had everyone take a break so that I could talk to him. He told me that he had a soccer game to go to and that he wasn't needed anyway. I realized I needed to explain to him that he needed to stay to be part of the team. I specifically explained to him that even though he was not a contributing member of the meeting it was important to stay to listen, learn, and show that he is committed to the team and its workload. Moreover, I let him know it was inappropriate to interrupt the meeting to inform us that he had to leave early because it disrupted the flow of the meeting. I tried to use this opportunity to teach him something about the importance and etiquette of meetings.

Do Not Make Inappropriate Comments. Jokes, erroneous statements, life stories, and so on are not appropriate in a meeting. In other words, never speak about anything that your mother would be ashamed to hear come out of your mouth. Although your comment may be innocent, others may interpret it as offensive. This will lead to trouble for your career sooner or later.

Do Not Speak about Politics, Religion, Sex, or Other Potentially Offensive Subjects. While such conversations may appear harmless, they can have damaging effects. By making certain comments, you may unknowingly alienate yourself from coworkers or managers. Avoid citing your political affiliations; they have no place in meetings. More importantly, these comments could subject you and the company to legal liability.

Do Not Let Your Emotions Get the Better of You. There is a big difference between discussion and argument. Always discuss, never argue. You will encounter argumentative situations later in your career, but they should not be occurring now. In fact, take measures to ensure that they do not. If a meeting becomes heated and you feel yourself becoming emotional, excuse yourself from the meeting. It is better to leave a meeting than to demonstrate inappropriate emotions.

> *There will be times when you will not have the answer to the question by the date/time you stated. Communicate with the person(s) that you need more time to provide an answer.*
>
> *By proactively stating you have not yet found an answer, the persons involved will know that you have not forgotten about their needs. This will also provide them with an opportunity to let you know if they no longer need the answer.*

ESSENTIALS OF BEING A FACILITATOR

The time will come, sooner than you think, when you will be required to facilitate a team or project meeting. When that time arrives, do not be apprehensive about it. Rather, view the experience as an opportunity to progress in your career. This is the best time to learn from your mistakes. Finally, it is also time for you to shine and to show your manager that you are willing to take on difficult tasks and go the extra mile.

Being a meeting facilitator is not easy. It will take time and experience for you to become comfortable in this role. However, at this stage of your career you should not let the prospect of being a meeting facilitator cause you undue stress. Your corporation, manager, mentor, and coworkers know that you are new to the business world. They will assist you to ensure that your first time as a facilitator is successful because your failure would reflect poorly on them.

Equally important, it is important for you to know that being the facilitator brings with it two major responsibilities—knowing when it is appropriate to set up a meeting and who to invite.

Even though meetings are an essential component in all organizations they can start to become what's wrong with organizations. Workers and organizations start to have a culture where meetings are needed to make all decisions; moreover, the meetings become dysfunctional and a waste of time. This is why it is important that you only set up a meeting if it is needed. If you can pick up the phone or send an e-mail to get the answer then do so. Moreover, if the meeting is finished early then dismiss your attendees. This will allow for them to go back and do necessary work.

Equally important, only invite the key players to the meeting. Invite people who are necessary for the education or decision-making process. This will ensure that you do not waste management and your coworkers' time. If someone that you included believes he or she needs another person at the meeting, encourage that individual to invite the person. Ensure that you take this responsibility seriously.

Plan the Meeting

The list that follows gives you an idea of just how much planning goes into a meeting. As you can see, a meeting is something that cannot just be thrown together at the last minute. However, do not panic. Just breathe, relax, and tackle the items that follow in turn:

- Book a meeting room that will accommodate all your attendees.

- Send a meeting invitation to all attendees.

> *Never, never, ever schedule a meeting during lunchtime unless you have approval from someone with higher authority than you or it is part of the company's culture. Most people need to eat and relax for a few minutes a day and lunchtime is personal time.*
> *You will know when you have the authority to set up a lunch meeting.*

- If you are unsure who to invite to the meeting, ask your mentor or an experienced coworker.

- When scheduling a same-day meeting, ensure all of your attendees are appropriately notified of the meeting (e-mail, phone call, or personal visit).

- Reserve any required meeting tools (projector, TV, DVD, microphone, etc.).

- Give yourself time prior to the meeting to familiarize yourself with the meeting tools. Ensure that all required meeting tools are functioning properly.

- Where possible, it is important to be mindful and considerate of the needs of your attendees when planning your meeting. Remember, meetings are a team effort; nothing is accomplished if attendees are uncomfortable, unprepared, or absent.

- Review your attendees' calendars to see if your meeting will unnecessarily interfere with their work schedules.

- Do not schedule your meeting as the fourth meeting in a row, unless there is no alternative.

- Early morning meetings are subject to the morning routine of your attendees (driving children to school, traffic, morning coffee, etc.).

> Do not schedule multiple meetings
> for the same day unless it is an
> absolute emergency.

If your meeting is large and will require extensive preparation time, designate sufficient time in your calendar to handle all the details— and there are many.

Create an Agenda

As the facilitator, it is important that you create an agenda. An agenda allows you to use your meeting time wisely and productively. Divide the meeting into the main topics that need to be discussed. Allocate the necessary amount of time that needs to be spent on each topic. Include time at the end to recap the meeting. A recap should occur five minutes prior to the end of the meeting.

Be sure all attendees receive a copy of the agenda in time to review it *before* the meeting. This gives everyone time to ask you questions or correct any errors you might have made. You want your attendees to be fully prepared for the meeting. That is the only way to have a productive meeting.

Let people know that you will conduct a recap at the end of the meeting.

Sample Agenda

Date: 1/15/10

Agenda

Project 123865—Implementation of New CRM

Attendees: Adam Scholl, John Smith, Richard Hemel, Wanda Jones, Elizabeth Hess

Introductions—5 minutes

Discuss Purpose of Project—10 Minutes

Review Project Plan—10 Minutes

Recap Meeting—5 Minutes

Prepare Yourself

Because the facilitator's job is to keep the meeting focused and on schedule, it is necessary that you review all relevant documentation before the meeting to verify that you know all the relevant facts. It is important to make notes on questions and comments that you have for attendees. However, you want to ensure that you do not ask someone a difficult question during a meeting that could be considered a form of blindsiding. If you have specific questions, ask the person before the meeting to give him/her time to prepare.

Organize all the documentation that you will bring to your meeting. If you will be using any meeting tool, take a moment to review its setup and use prior to your scheduled meeting. Always try it out ahead of time to be sure it is working properly.

Create a Plan B in case your meeting tool does not work properly (i.e., have hard copies of your PowerPoint presentation). If difficulties arise in setting up a particular tool, at some point you must stop fiddling and move the meeting along. You should not delay the meeting for more than 5 minutes to get a meeting tool working; moreover, if you have become flustered over the delay then inform the attendees that it is necessary to reschedule the meeting. Apologize to your attendees for cancelling the meeting. It is better to delay a meeting than to be a facilitator of a poor meeting.

> As long as it does not unnecessarily waste time, you may briefly review a document during a meeting to retrieve an answer but it is much better to review all documents before the meeting.

Prepare Your Attendees

Just as your own preparation is tied to the success of your meeting, so is the preparation of your attendees. It is your responsibility to ensure they have everything they need to actively participate and contribute to your meeting. You cannot have a meeting to discuss the company's budget proposal for the next fiscal year if your attendees have not had sufficient time to review it. To ensure their adequate preparation, do the following:

- Send all necessary meeting documentation at least two business days before the scheduled meeting date.
- If there is a large volume of these materials, allocate additional time.
- Send the agenda to the attendees prior to the meeting.

Facilitation

Arrive early to set up your computer, pass out your handouts, clean the white board, remove any clutter from the conference room, and do other preparations.

Begin the meeting by introducing yourself and going over your agenda for the meeting. Next, have all meeting attendees introduce themselves if it is appropriate.

As the meeting facilitator, it is your responsibility to manage the meeting. Do not let the meeting lose focus. If discussions occur that are not relevant, stop those discussions politely by reiterating what is on the agenda.

At the end of the meeting, do a short recap. Be sure to review all important facts and deliverables. Do the recap at least five minutes prior to the meeting's ending.

Have someone critique your meeting. In addition to being a great learning tool, this extra step also gives the appearance that you are a professional and care about the quality of your work. Ask a respected co-worker to critique how effectively you handled your meeting. Listen and discuss any issues that this person brings to your attention. Do not take offense to any of the feedback that the person provides to you.

Do not let a meeting tool run the meeting. Meeting tools, such as PowerPoint, are not intended to run the meeting for you. They are intended to assist you in staying on track and to assist your attendees in following along. They are not intended to act as your primary source for information. Your primary source is your inner voice, so let it sing.

Do not waste the attendees' time. Nothing aggravates people more quickly than the realization that their time is being wasted. While meetings are important, you need to be careful not to waste time. Here are a few simple rules to ensure your meeting remains productive and on track:

- Do not show up late or take time out during the meeting to correct a problem with a meeting tool.

- If a meeting tool is not working after a few minutes, continue your meeting without it.

- If you complete the meeting's agenda with time to spare, conduct your recap and dismiss everyone. Remember, your attendees have other work they need to be doing.

- Know the right people to invite and invite them. In other words, do not invite everyone.

Personal Account

It is important that the facilitator control the meeting. This control comes in many forms: the flow of information, questions, and answers, the speed of discussion. If you do not control the tone, the meeting will become unproductive and also could lead to you becoming known as an ineffective leader/facilitator.

I was conducting a meeting that was intense. By the time this meeting came around, I was a solid facilitator of conveyance and decision-making meetings; however, I had never encountered a meeting in which the discussion disintegrated into personal jabs. I knew I had to take control immediately. I did this by asking both persons to stop and then stating that this type of behavior was not acceptable. Furthermore, I told everyone to take a 10-minute break during which I talked to both employees. Once the meeting was over, I documented the incident and forwarded the information to my manager to ensure that the company was protected.

IN CONCLUSION

Meetings are an important component of the business culture. In this chapter, we discussed the two types of meetings: corporate conveyance and decision-making meetings. Furthermore, the chapter provided important information on how to be a facilitator. All of this information has given you the framework to understand and master meetings.

More important, in keeping with the theme of this book, this chapter further illustrates and articulates that being a professional is a complex endeavor. Having the right education and credentials are not enough. To be a professional requires you to understand not only the most complex business functions, but the basic business functions such as *meetings*. Ensure that you take the basics from this chapter and employ them.

4

TRAVELING FOR WORK

Do your duty and a little more and the future will take care of itself.

—ANDREW CARNEGIE

CHAPTER CONCEPTS

Essentials to a Successful
Travel Experience

Dynamics of Office Visits

Actions to Avoid While Traveling

ESSENTIALS TO A SUCCESSFUL TRAVEL EXPERIENCE

Depending on your position within a corporation, part of your job might require you to travel. Regardless of whether you perceive traveling as an inconvenience or a perk, you must be a professional at all times while traveling because you represent your corporation. Because of this, you need to carefully review and understand your corporation's policies on employee work-related travel so that you do not break any corporate rules. Although these corporate policies will explain what you should do, they will probably not explain the essentials of a successful travel experience. The following sections have been provided to fill this gap. Remember, it is always better to be a leader than a follower!

Review Corporate Travel Policies. This is an absolute must before you travel for any work-related assignments. This will ensure that you know your corporations rules when traveling on behalf of your company. And hopefully the policies will answer any questions you may have and possibly bring issues to light that you did not think of. However, if you have any outstanding questions after reading your corporate travel policies then contact your superior or the human resources department prior to your departure. You do not want to travel for your company until you know what they expect of you.

> *Talk to a respected coworker who has traveled for the company before. He or she will be able to expand on the ins and outs of the company's travel policies.*

Making Travel Arrangements. If your company has a travel department, they will probably want them to make your travel arrangements for you. This department will make your travel arrangements based on corporate policies so you will have little say on flight times, hotel locations, car rentals, and so on. However, this does not mean you can't ask for any special arrangements. Just make sure that you get your manager's prior approval and that you have a valid reason for the special arrangements.

If you are making your own travel arrangements then you need to take the following into consideration:

- Air transportation—If you need to book a flight then get the cheapest flight. There is no reason for your company to pay extra for first class, business class, or a more expensive flight just because it is twenty minutes shorter. However, this does not mean that you need to book a flight that makes your travel experience difficult and stressful. It just means that you need to justify to yourself, and possibly your company, why you chose a flight that was more expensive. Make sure to take into consideration any layovers when you are booking flights. Remember, flights are often late and some airports, like Atlanta, are large so it takes some time to get to connecting gates. Give yourself at least one hour between connecting flights so that you do not miss your flight.

- Hotel accommodations—It is important that you book a hotel that has a reasonable rate but also allows for you to relax after a long day of work. And let me stress this point—when you travel for work you will work long days because you will need to accomplish a lot of work in a short period of time. Hence, picking the right hotel room is important so consider the following when booking a hotel room:

  —Location. Take into consideration the proximity of the hotel to your work site. You do not want to spend an hour driving to and from a work site because this will only cause unnecessary stress. Equally important, take into consideration the location of your hotel to restaurants, grocery stores, and so on. The last thing you will want to do is search for a restaurant late at night in a city that you do not know well.

—Safety. Ensure that the hotel is in a secure location. Your safety comes first so ask persons at work or persons you will be visiting if a specific location is safe.

—Hotel amenities. It is important that your hotel offer certain basics. First, pick a hotel that offers a good breakfast that is served during hours that work for you. Second, ensure that the hotel rooms offer a desk and chair in their rooms because you will need a place to work. Third, free internet access. Fourth, free parking unless it is unavoidable. Fifth, an iron for your use because you will need it. Last, make sure that your hotel has a business center even if you are bringing your laptop—trust me, it will come in handy.

• Ground transportation consists of car rental and taxi.

—Car rental. If you have to rent a vehicle, consider the following: First, pick a vehicle that you will feel comfortable driving in a strange city. Second, if you will be driving a lot consider renting a navigational system. Third, some company policies require their employees not to pay for car rental insurance because the company is self-insured so know your company's rules. Fourth, make sure that you return the vehicle on time. Moreover, pay attention to what actions you need to take when returning the vehicle. For instance, do you need to fill up the gas tank prior to returning the vehicle? Last, if more than one person will be using the vehicle ensure that this information is in the rental agreement.

—Taxi. If it is more economical to use a taxi or car service, make sure that you consider the following: Use a licensed service. Second, ensure that the taxi accepts credit cards and gives receipts prior to getting into the cab. Last, ensure that you do not leave anything in the taxi.

> *Orbitz.com, Expedia.com, and Priceline.com are all great websites for booking hotels, and air and ground transportation.*

Meals on Your Company's Dime. Make sure to eat within your allotted per diem or allowance for daily meals. Just because you are traveling on behalf or your company does not mean you have the right to eat at the most expensive place. Furthermore, employees need to be conscious of all costs, which includes the cost of meals. Moreover, if your company has not stated a per diem, then use the following rules as guidelines:

$10 to $15 per day for breakfast

$15 to $20 per day for lunch

$25 to $30 per day for dinner

Use the low range numbers when you travel to cities that are not as expensive and the higher range values for more expensive cities. The above values do not include tips so include a tip that is not more than 15 percent.

Per diem

An allowance for daily expenses, such as meals.

In addition to cost, you need to be mindful of choosing a reputable place to eat. For instance, eating at Hooters on the company's dime is not appropriate because some within your company will believe Hooter's business model objectifies women. Again, this is your career, so making smart choices about where you eat will ensure that you do not run into obstacles that can be avoided.

> *True professionals are always cost conscious, treating the company's money as they would treat their own.*

Attire. Your company's dress code should be followed when you travel. In fact, it is important that you represent your company in such a manner that your work product will be reviewed—not your appearance.

Remember the white socks and clip-on tie personal story. Be careful to dress in a way that showcases your professionalism. Also be aware of the dress codes of the company you are visiting. If they are less formal than your company, resist switching to their style. You are still representing your company.

Travel Documents. Make sure that you review and print out copies of all your business travel documents, which include:

- Travel and meeting agendas,
- Flight information,
- Hotel reservation,
- Car rental information or who will pick you up at the airport, and
- Printed driving instructions from the airport to the hotel and to the meeting place.

Reviewing your travel documents and familiarizing yourself with your travel itinerary will help to ease any pre-travel jitters and ensure that you have everything you need to complete a successful trip.

Pre-Departure Work Tasks. Traveling can be stressful and tiring, not to mention all the added concerns you might feel from being absent from the office for the duration of your trip. In order to alleviate some of these additional anxieties, set aside enough time for the following tasks on the day before you leave:

- Set your e-mail system to automatically notify others that you will be out of the office. Make sure that you include in the notification the dates you will be out of the office and who should be contacted in case of an emergency.

- Set your voice-mail system to notify others that you will be out of the office. State in your message when you will be returning to the office. Make sure your voice-mail message identifies someone the caller may contact in case of an emergency.

- Make a notification in your calendar when you will be out of the office.

- Place a sign in your office that lets others know you are out of the office.

- Personally notify close coworkers and superiors that you will be out of town.

- Catch up with e-mail and regular mail prior to departing.

> *Notifying close coworkers of your absence will help to eliminate confusion while you are gone; furthermore, it will let your coworkers know that you are part of the team.*

Ending Your Trip Professionally. Allow yourself enough time at the end of your trip to recap your visit with your hosts and to make your scheduled transportation. When recapping your visit, it is important that you thank your hosts for their hospitality, discuss the action items that have been completed, and the actions that need to still be researched. This will ensure that all parties are the on same page in knowing what has been done and what still needs to be done. Equally important, ensure that you do not rush to the airport. Inform your hosts up front of your departure time so that you do not miss your flight home.

Expense Report. Filling out and returning an expense report is part of your duties when you travel for a corporation. While this process can be very time-consuming, it is necessary that you finish the report in a timely manner. It is also equally important that you fill the form out correctly. This means you need to dedicate at least 30 minutes for completing the form for every week the expense report represents. You may find that you have time on the return flight to start this task.

By following the simple steps listed next, completing your expense report will be much easier:

- Keep all of your *itemized* receipts and immediately write the name of the establishment, city, state, date, and persons paid on the back of the receipt.

- Remember, it is not appropriate to bill alcohol or tobacco products to your company.

- Make sure to keep track of the receipts.

- Photocopy the front/back of all receipts for your own records.

- Fill out the necessary travel forms and keep a copy for your own records.

- If the corporate credit card statement is mailed to you, make sure to recheck the expenses on the bill against your records.

SAMPLE EXPENSE REPORT

Date:_____

Name: _____

Employee ID: _____

Purpose of Expenditures: _____

Dates of Expenditures:_____

Department:_____

Reporting Manager:_____

Date

Description

Persons Covered

Cost

Total

Manager Signature:_____

Employee Signature:_____

It is important that you fill out and return your expense report in a timely manner.

DYNAMICS OF OFFICE VISITS

When you travel for your company, you will either travel to a satellite office, a customer's location, a supplier's location, or to a convention. The dynamics of each of these travel sites will be different. So, it is important to understand the dynamics and how to approach the visits so that you are prepared.

Satellite Office. There may be many reasons for you to visit a satellite office: the launch of a new product, a yearly employee meeting, to attend training or conduct training, and so on. However, no matter what the reason may be, when traveling to a satellite office it is important that you understand that you are a guest and act accordingly. When visiting a satellite office, ensure that you respect their established rules and also their unofficial office rules. For instance, it may be okay at your location to talk on a cell phone while at your desk but this may not be the case at the satellite office. So take a moment to ask your host the rules of the office.

Equally important, there is an expectation that when you travel to a satellite office that you stay connected to your office. In other words, while traveling to a satellite office it is your responsibility to check e-mail and voice mail at least four times a day: early morning, mid-morning, lunch, mid-afternoon, and at the close of business day. Moreover, while checking your e-mail and voice mail during this time, you need to respond to any important e-mails or voice mail. Equally important, if you have an emergency then you need to inform your host that there is a problem at your office and that you need to take care of it. Your host will understand that your duties at your primary site are as important as the duties that you are performing at the satellite office.

Customer. Visiting a customer's site can be difficult but it is important that you always stay professional. You may visit a customer site for many reasons: finalizing a business contract, training, reviewing a defect with your product, and so on. Some of these reasons can be easier to handle while others, such as having a discussion with a customer about why your product is failing to meet quality control standards, can be difficult. These difficult visits will test your professionalism and will cause great stress at times but it is your responsibility and your duty as an advocate for your company to always stay professional—no matter what.

I recommend that while visiting customer sites you employ the age-old approach that the customer is always right. (Customers are not always right for your company but you are not in the position to determine when the customer should no longer be a customer.) This does not mean that you cannot disagree with your customer; it just means that you always need to understand their problem and work to resolve it. By incorporating this approach in your critical thinking, you will not take their criticisms personally and you will not forget that you are on site to solve a problem for your customer. Moreover, customers are fully aware that no product or service is perfect so they do understand that problems occur; they are just looking for suppliers that care. By putting the customer first, you will win over your customers in the long run.

Supplier. Visiting suppliers will not be as difficult as visiting a customer but, again, it is important that you remain professional at all times. When visiting suppliers it is important to stay on point and to be an advocate for your company. You should not accept any gifts from anyone nor drink alcohol while visiting a supplier. Moreover, even though you are the customer, do not act in such a way that makes them decide it is no longer worth it to have you as a customer.

Conventions. Conventions are a time to network and to be educated. It is important that you are professional at all times because you will be representing your corporation and your actions can have a negative connotation for your corporation. So enjoy but be professional.

ACTIONS TO AVOID WHILE TRAVELING

While it is important to give you a set of guidelines for traveling for work, it is even more important that you are aware of the actions to avoid. When traveling, you represent your company, so I strongly urge you to pay very close attention to a number of important suggestions.

Do Not Speak Negatively about Your Company. Never speak negatively about your company to anyone during your travels. You can never be sure who the person you are speaking to knows or represents. In addition, you can never be sure who might be listening to your conversation. Trust me, the business world is smaller than you think, and word travels fast.

Do Not Lose Your Cool. It is extremely important that you keep your composure at all times. The best way to ensure an even disposition is to avoid becoming intoxicated when traveling on business.

Do Not Eat at Inappropriate Places. Be careful not to eat at establishments that would offend others. There are many neutrally themed restaurants from which to select.

> *If you simply cannot resist the temptation to eat at an inappropriate restaurant, pay for the meal out of your own pocket.*

Do Not Charge Alcohol to Your Company. Under no circumstance should you ever charge alcohol to your corporation. Most restaurants will put alcohol purchases on a separate receipt if you request it. If you are in a position that requires you to wine and dine clients, then, and only then, is it appropriate to charge alcohol to your corporation.

> *The best idea is not to drink alcohol while traveling for your company. This will ensure that you are professional at all times.*

Do Not Charge Expenses to Your Hotel Room. Do not charge anything to the room at your company's expense, except for room service that falls within your per diem. If you need to make a charge to your room then pay for the expense out of your own pocket. This includes spa services and in-room videos.

Do Not Accept Gifts. You never want to accept gifts while you are representing your company or corporation. This includes someone buying you a beer, a meal, giving you leftover product, and so on.

Do Not Have Inappropriate Relations. It is not appropriate to have sexual relations with business associates that you are traveling with, or with individuals who are employed at your temporary work site. Remember, this is your career, so be smart and resist the temptation.

IN CONCLUSION

If you travel on company business, it is important that you take your duties seriously and be professional at all times. Make sure to always talk positively about your company, track your expenses, and make wise decisions while traveling. Furthermore, take the right actions prior to traveling for work. Last, understand your role and the dynamics of the place you are traveling to so that you are prepared for the unexpected. Remember, this is your career so being a professional while traveling on behalf of your corporation is a must.

CHAPTER 5

CAREER GROWTH

By working faithfully eight hours a day you may eventually get to be boss and work twelve hours a day.

—ROBERT FROST

In the business world, everyone is paid in two coins: cash and experience. Take the experience first; the cash will come later.

—HAROLD S. GENEEN

CHAPTER CONCEPTS

Pay Attention to Your Career
Growth Now

Is An Online Degree Right for
You?

Track Your Own Progress

Asking for a Raise/Promotion

Résumé

PAY ATTENTION TO YOUR CAREER GROWTH NOW

We enter the corporate world with grand visions of becoming the company CEO the following day. Well, that simply does not happen. However, it is possible one day to become the CEO, CFO, president, director, or supervisor, if you begin to take your career seriously today. By exercising initiative and taking control of your career growth now, you will ensure that no opportunities for career advancement slip through your fingers.

> *Taking your career seriously today will allow you to develop a greater appreciation of the dynamics involved in advancing your career to the next level.*

Achieving career growth and avoiding career stagnation, which occurs when you treat your current position as a *job* not a career, requires personal determination and hard work. You have to realize that your career is just that—yours! No person or company will hold your hand all the way up to the position of CEO. It is up to you to make the most of your career and to determine the best approach to achieving your career goals. The following discussion outlines some of the tasks you can perform to take charge of your career now and ensure that it will prosper and grow.

Develop Goals

One of the most effective techniques is to develop and work toward your own set of goals. You should develop both short- and long-term goals. Moreover, you need to develop both personal and professional goals because you need to make certain that they align. For instance, if you have a personal goal of obtaining a doctorate in business then you need to ensure that your business goals include aspects that will guarantee your acceptance into a PhD program—being published in journals, authoring books, gaining leadership and corporate experience, and so on. Furthermore, your personal goals can impact your professional career such as getting an advanced degree.

Use the following information in creating and maintaining your personal and professional goals:

- Do not select goals that are impossible to achieve.
- Do not select goals that are too easy to achieve.
- Do not create an excessive number of goals.
- Keep your goals short and concise.
- Constantly review, evaluate, and update your progress.

Find Professional Mentors

A mentor is a trusted counselor or guide. This definition is right on; however, I think it is important to discuss two points. First, the definition includes the word trusted which is important because you need to trust your mentor. There will be many moments in your career where it will be necessary for you to be able to speak to your mentor about subjects that require discretion. Second, you need to pick mentors who are able to counsel or guide you in making career decisions which means they need to be seasoned professionals. However, this does not mean they have to be in your career track, it just means that they need to be professionals who are seasoned enough in their career track to be able to guide you in your career. Moreover, I urge you to have mentors who are outside of your career track so that you can make decisions based on advice that is cross-discipline. You need mentors to grow your career because they will be able to guide you through unknown territory.

Continuing Education

The dynamics of the business world are constantly changing. There is a good chance that some of the techniques you learned in your early college years may already have become obsolete by the time you graduated from college. Thus, it is very important that you continue to build your formal education, which you can do in the following ways:

- Attend professional seminars and workshops.
- Acquire certifications and advanced degrees.
- Attend lectures given by prominent speakers.
- Review relevant books and published articles.
- Become an instructor at a college or university.

It is important that you understand that as a professional it is your responsibility to continue to improve and expand your knowledge base. This will require you to educate yourself outside of the work environment; moreover, it is your responsibility to invest in your career by purchasing books and paying for seminars even if your corporation will not.

> *Get a subscription to at least two magazines or journals that are not in your professional track because it will help develop your critical thinking and it will broaden your knowledge base.*

IS AN ONLINE DEGREE RIGHT FOR YOU?

Many educational institutions now offer online degrees so you need to spend the necessary time researching the pros and cons of obtaining an online degree. While you conduct your research, consider the following questions:

1. Is the purpose to obtain your first undergraduate degree? If you are already in the corporate community and have not obtained your undergraduate degree then receiving a degree online is fine. At this point in your career, you are acquiring a tool that is necessary in your tool belt for corporate advancement.

2. Are you obtaining an advanced degree for the purpose of advancing your career? You need to determine if an online degree is the right environment for you. Moreover, you need to determine if online degrees are accepted in your discipline.

3. Are you earning an advanced degree for the purpose of being an educator at the university level? If this is your intention then an online degree is probably not the right choice because online degrees are not given the same authority as degrees obtained at brick-and-mortar schools. This attitude may change as the quality of schools offering online degrees changes.

4. Is the school accredited? Any school that you attend must be at least accredited by one of the six regional accreditation institutions.

5. Do you believe that you may move within the next year or obtain a new position? Then an

online degree will provide you the necessary flexibility that will be required.

While keeping these questions in mind, you also need to consider what your business community thinks of online degrees. The majority of businesses and professionals believe that an online undergraduate degree obtained from an accredited institution is equivalent, for the most part, to traditional degrees obtained from a brick-and-mortar school. However, online advanced degrees are perceived to hold less authority then traditional advanced degrees obtained from brick-and-mortar schools although this attitude may be changing. It is important that you do the necessary research before you obtain an online degree.

> *It is your responsibility to continue to educate yourself in your chosen career.*

TRACK YOUR OWN PROGRESS

Half the battle of your career growth is accurately tracking your progress. It is important that you keep track of your career progress for a number of reasons. In this chapter, I have outlined what I believe to be the three most important justifications for tracking the progress of your career growth.

Nobody Will Do This for You

First and foremost, no other person in your organization will keep track of your progress. Yes, it is true that your supervisors and colleagues will know if you are a competent employee. However, this does not necessarily mean that your career decision makers will fully understand your career accomplishments. This is why it is important that you keep track of your specific accomplishments so that you can refer to them when seeking a raise, promotion, or as a guide for future work.

Past Experience

Second, tracking your career progress will ensure that you do not forget your past career accomplishments. Inevitably, as time passes in your career, you will forget specific tasks you have accomplished that illustrate the level of your current operational abilities. And when the time comes to ask for the promotion, your managers will ask for examples of work you have done that proves you should get the promotion.

Know Your Strengths and Weaknesses

Third, tracking your career progress will provide you with the necessary information to understand and acknowledge your career strengths and weaknesses, which you can use to further your career. Once you know your weaknesses, you can formulate a plan to minimize them. One important way to assess your organization's perception of your strengths and weaknesses is through performance reviews.

TRACKING YOUR PROGRESS

Tracking your career progress will allow you to have all the necessary information at your disposal to effectively advocate for yourself when pursuing a promotion. Moreover, you will not have to try and put together your information at the last minute when you are trying to advance your career.

As discussed, tracking your own career progress is very important. This process can be relatively easy, provided you have a good action plan at your disposal. The following suggestions will make your life much easier when tracking the progression of your career:

- Develop two folders that you will use to save your work: an electronic copy and a paper copy.

- Save every memo and e-mail that you create that illustrates your strengths and weaknesses. Make sure that you file them in a manner that will allow you to easily find specific memos.

- Create a spreadsheet that contains your current job duties and the job duties of the position that you want. Keep track within the spreadsheet of which job duties you are performing. More-over, make sure to provide yourself enough details in the spreadsheet so that you can refer back to the example in a more detailed manner if need be.

- Spend at least one hour a month reviewing and updating your spreadsheet.

- Equally important, make sure to save any com-munications that provide positive feedback from managers and coworkers.

PERFORMANCE REVIEWS

A performance review is the process management uses to provide feedback on your performance in your cur-rent position for a stated period of time. This assess-ment provides information about whether you are meeting or not meeting the companies' expectations for your current position. This will allow you to deter-mine areas in your career that you can grow. Equally important, performance reviews are used to determine promotions and raises. This is why it is important to take performance reviews seriously.

It may appear you do not have much control over your performance reviews but that is not the case. Yes, your manager does fill out your performance re-view but you control your performance! Most man-agers, even incompetent managers, will not score you low out of spite because even incompetent managers realize that they need professionals on their team. So, by being a professional you will control your performance review. Moreover, the following steps will aid you in ensuring that your performance review is a positive career growth experience.

First, it is important that you understand your company's performance review process. Every company has a different performance review process and it is important that you take the necessary time to become familiar with your company's process so that you are prepared. For instance, consider the following questions:

- Do your coworkers and other managers fill out pre-determined questionnaires evaluating your performance?

- Does just your manager evaluate your performance?

- Do you fill out a self-evaluation form?

- Do you get you a copy of the evaluation prior to your performance review meeting?

- Is your performance review used for promotions and/or raises?

- Do you have a 90-day performance review? A yearly performance review?

> *It is important that you find out whether your company has a 90-day review process because this may mean that you have a probationary period with the company when you start.*

These are just a few questions that you need to have answered prior to your performance review. Moreover, make sure that you understand what is expected of you on the day of your performance review. You can obtain all of this information from your manager, human resource representative, and coworkers.

Second, you need to determine if you believe it is time for a promotion or a raise by reviewing your career growth–tracking spreadsheet. Gather specific work examples that re-enforce your job performance— this should be easy since you have been tracking your career growth. After gathering your specific work examples, take time to write a narrative of your work accomplishments. This will allow you to prepare how to recap your performance for the time period and ask for your promotion or raise. Last, relax, listen, and be an advocate for yourself during your evaluation.

Finally, recap and adjust if necessary. After you and your manager meet for your performance review, it is necessary that you recap and adjust. Take the necessary time after your review to recap what you and your manager discussed. Furthermore, write down specific improvements or deliverables that your manager requested from you. Moreover, if necessary, adjust your professional goals to address any improvements. Take this time to honestly adjust your performance so that your career stays on an upward path.

What if you receive a negative performance review? Having some categories or areas that your manager identifies as areas that you need to improve is not a bad performance review. Put it in perspective—all professionals need to improve in areas in their job description or they need to be promoted. If you have more than two categories or areas in which your manager indicated below average performance then your performance review was bad. Now, this does not mean you are going to be fired or that you are not a professional. (I would argue if you are reading this section in this book then you are a professional because you want to improve yourself!) What it does mean is that you need to honestly review what your manager said and what this means. You need to decide if your current position is right for you. Furthermore, determine if you can make the necessary changes in a time frame that allows you to maintain your current position. Last, do not spend your time worrying about getting fired; instead spend your time improving your skill set.

ASKING FOR A RAISE/PROMOTION

A corporation will not go out of its way to offer you a raise and/or a promotion unless there is a vacancy that needs to be filled. Corporations have set times when raises are made and when to consider employees for promotions. Again, this period is most likely during your performance review as stated earlier in this chapter. However, this does not mean you should sit and wait for a promotion to be offered to you. It is up to you to ensure that you are compensated and recognized for your contributions to the company.

Asking for a promotion and pay raise can be daunting. This is understandable given that you are advocating for yourself, which can be a difficult undertaking. However, the following suggestions should ease the process.

Assess Position Qualifications

Determine the exact qualifications required for the position and use those as the subject of your promotion request. Knowing these qualifications will allow you to set work goals. Moreover, it will allow you to showcase completed work that is aligned with the duties of the position you are trying to obtain.

Track Career Progression

Keeping track of your career progression, as described in the previous section, will help you determine when you are able to perform the tasks of your next desired career position, which in return will allow you to gauge when you should ask for a promotion. Moreover, this will allow you to provide detailed information to your manager about why you deserve a promotion.

Organization and Presentation

Ensure that you gather and organize your career progression material in a manner that will allow you to professionally present it to the persons making the decision on your promotion or raise. Make sure to provide enough material for them to take with them along with a concise narrative of your accomplishments.

The 35 Percent Rule

Once you have performed or are performing 35 percent of the work involved in the next position in your career growth progression ladder, set up an appointment to *discuss* your career advancement. This discussion will put your manager on notice that you are working toward a promotion and it will also allow you to receive some feedback regarding any deficiencies in garnering the promotion.

Continuous Improvement

Ensure that you make a conscious effort to improve on any deficiencies discussed in your performance reviews. Equally important, make sure that you keep track of any positive steps that you may have taken in correcting any stated deficiencies so that you can bring this to the attention of management when discussing a raise or a promotion.

Be Confident

When you discuss your raise/promotion with your reporting supervisor make sure that you are confident. There is a fine line between being confident and arrogant. Make sure that you are the former not the latter.

RÉSUMÉ

You must always be ready for the unexpected. This can include layoffs, termination, career transition, or an internal promotion within your current company. In the business community it is always prudent to have a current résumé. The difficulty in keeping your résumé current is remembering to keep it updated. As long as you remember to make periodic updates, everything else will be relatively easy.

The following is a list of steps you can take to ensure your résumé is updated and ready at a moment's notice:

- Develop and maintain specific résumés for specific careers.

- Ensure that you update/modify your résumé on noncorporate assets.

- Do not modify your résumé while at work.

- Schedule time once a quarter to update your résumé.

- Review current industry standards and practices to determine if you need to modify the style of your résumé.

- Modify your résumé according to your career growth.

> It is also important to maintain an online business profile such as LinkedIn. Your Facebook or Myspace profile do not count.

This chapter is not intended to explain how to create a résumé but to ensure that you continue to update your résumé with current information. There are many good reference books on writing résumés. Be sure to use them when you construct your résumé. An example of a good résumé that you can use to guide you is on the next page.

Adam Scholl

Phone Number * *Physical Address* * *E-mail Address*

BUSINESS SYSTEM ANALYST

Hands-on leader with extensive product development, analysis and management expertise in . . .

Core Competencies

Product Architecture, Engineering, Development • Decision Making • Statements of Work • . . .

PROFESSIONAL EXPERIENCE

Raymond James Financial, Inc., St. Petersburg, Florida
Start Date—End Date
Raymond James is a Fortune 1,000 financial services holding company with subsidiaries engaged in investment and financial planning, investment banking and asset management.

Lead Business Analyst | Project Manager (Consultant)
Led project to upgrade customer management application using waterfall approach, Borland solutions and UML models; project goal was to add . . .

Publix Super Markets, Inc., Lakeland, Florida
Start Date—End Date
Founded in 1930, Fortune 500 company Publix Super Markets is the largest and fastest-growing employee-owned supermarket chain in the United States.

System Analyst/Programmer
. . .
Key Projects Include:
. . . .

(continued on next page)

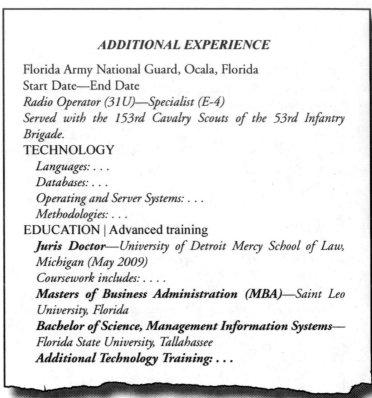

ADDITIONAL EXPERIENCE

Florida Army National Guard, Ocala, Florida
Start Date—End Date
Radio Operator (31U)—Specialist (E-4)
Served with the 153rd Cavalry Scouts of the 53rd Infantry Brigade.
TECHNOLOGY
  Languages: . . .
  Databases: . . .
  Operating and Server Systems: . . .
  Methodologies: . . .
EDUCATION | Advanced training
  Juris Doctor—*University of Detroit Mercy School of Law, Michigan (May 2009)*
  Coursework includes: . . . .
  Masters of Business Administration (MBA)—*Saint Leo University, Florida*
  Bachelor of Science, Management Information Systems—*Florida State University, Tallahassee*
  Additional Technology Training: . . .

First, the résumé informs the reader who the applicant is and how to contact the person. This information will allow the interviewer to locate your contact information easily.

Second, it is important to include a concise paragraph explaining who you are with emphasis on your expertise in the position that you are trying to obtain.

BUSINESS SYSTEM ANALYST
Hands-on leader with extensive product development, analysis and management expertise in . . .

Third, it is important to highlight your core competencies because in this information technology age companies use programs to search for résumés. The core competencies section gives you a section to highlight your skill set to a reader and also to allow companies to use key search words to pull up your résumé.

Core Competencies
Product Architecture, Engineering, Development • Decision Making • Statements of Work • . . .

Fourth, add a professional experience section. Now that you have a professional résumé, your education is secondary to your professional experience. Make sure to include the names of the companies you worked for, a brief description of the company, and your start and end dates. Moreover, it is important to include the positions that you held and a description of your duties in a paragraph form. Ensure that you use proper grammar. Last, include key projects that you worked on while highlighting key success in the projects. This is the section where you want to highlight specifics of your success.

PROFESSIONAL EXPERIENCE

Raymond James Financial, Inc., St. Petersburg, Florida
Start Date—End Date
Raymond James is a Fortune 1,000 financial services holding company with subsidiaries engaged in investment and financial planning, investment banking and asset management.

Lead Business Analyst | Project Manager (Consultant)
Led project to upgrade customer management application using waterfall approach, Borland solutions and UML models; project goal was to add . . .

Publix Super Markets, Inc., Lakeland, Florida
Start Date—End Date
Founded in 1930, Fortune 500 company Publix Super Markets is the largest and fastest-growing employee-owned supermarket chain in the United States.

System Analyst/Programmer

. . .
Key Projects Include:

. . . .

Fifth, you may include an additional experience section for any additional professional experience that does not fit within the professional experience section, I emphasize *professional,* experience. For instance, I include my military experience in this section because it is experience that I am proud of and I want employers to know that I severed in the Florida Army National Guard. Furthermore, include any other sections that will emphasis your particular skill set for the career that you are trying to land.

ADDITIONAL EXPERIENCE

Florida Army National Guard, Ocala, Florida
Start Date—End Date
Radio Operator (31U)—Specialist (E-4)
Served with the 153rd Cavalry Scouts of the 53rd Infantry Brigade.
TECHNOLOGY
    Languages: . . .
    Databases: . . .
    Operating and Server Systems: . . .
    Methodologies: . . .

Last, include your education and advanced training. Start with your most recent education then work backward. Do not put the dates that you graduated because it takes away from your professional experience unless you need to show the gap in your professional experience.

EDUCATION | Advanced training
Juris Doctor—*University of Detroit Mercy School of Law,
Michigan (May 2009)*
Coursework includes: . . . .
Masters of Business Administration (MBA)—*Saint Leo
University, Florida*
Bachelor of Science, Management Information Systems—
Florida State University, Tallahassee
Additional Technology Training:
. . .

IN CONCLUSION

It is important that you take control of your career now so that you achieve your desired personal and professional goals. Make sure that you find professional mentors and continue to educate yourself. Moreover, start tracking the progression of your career now so that you are ready to advocate for yourself. Also, educate yourself on your company's performance review process so that you can track your career progression properly. Last, stay on top of your résumé to ensure that you are prepared to further your career at any time. Hence, you control your career growth so you need to take control of your career now.

6

HUMAN RESOURCES

If you pick the right people and give them the opportunity to spread their wings and put compensation as a carrier behind it, you almost don't have to manage them.

—JACK WELCH

CHAPTER CONCEPTS

What is an HR Department?

What Can HR Do for You?

Unacceptable Behavior

Sick Days

Vacation Time

Personal Time

How to Resign from
Your Position

WHAT IS A HUMAN RESOURCES DEPARTMENT?

The human resources (HR) department within a business is intended to be an advocate for both the corporation and its employees. It is developed and structured to ensure that the corporation's interests are protected, which automatically includes protecting and nurturing the interests of its employees because you are an asset. Human resources departments protect and develop corporate assets in many ways: finding human capital, developing human capital, providing a safe work environment, and so on. However, every HR department functions a bit differently, so you need to get familiar with the procedures and processes your HR department uses.

To accomplish its main goal of protecting the corporation's interests, the HR department is required to enforce corporate rules, state and federal laws, and so on. This is why lawyers are frequently chosen to be the head of HR departments. It is hoped that their understanding of the law will allow them to guide the department. Sometimes, enforcing these laws results in the HR department having a negative connotation because employees and management perceive this department to be the enemy. This attitude and mentality is wrong and should be avoided. The HR department is protecting the interests of all employees by enforcing these rules. Furthermore, the HR department does not fire people; people fire themselves by not being professional.

The HR department re-enforces corporate rules, state and federal laws, and so on by making continuing education available. Most of the information the HR department will provide to you is designed to keep you from breaking any rules that could result in your termination. This why it is important for you to engage your HR department and take all of their correspondence seriously. Equally important, engaging the HR department allows you to feel comfortable utilizing their services in the event you need their help.

Again, I cannot stress it enough: the HR department is your advocate. They ensure that you and your fellow coworkers are comfortable performing your daily duties while protecting the company's interests.

> *Get to know your HR representative by stopping by and introducing yourself.*

WHAT CAN HUMAN RESOURCES DO FOR YOU?

The HR department, as your advocate, will work to ensure you are treated in a professional manner by seeing that both management and other company employees follow all corporate policies. By performing this task, the HR department makes it clear to all company employees that they are all working on the same level. While past experience has taught me that it is possible for special or negative treatment by HR personnel to occur, this is the exception and not the rule.

Although the HR department is your advocate, this does not mean that it will always have all the necessary information to perform its job to the fullest. Thus, you should take the following actions to ensure that the HR department will be able to act as your advocate:

- Keep HR informed of any certificates, awards, achievements, or other honors that you receive.

- Maintain a folder that contains all general and personal HR-related documentation.

- Respond to all HR inquires professionally and in a timely manner.

- Do not speak negatively about the HR department.

- Keep an accurate record of sick days, personal days, vacation days, holiday time, tardiness, and any other work time that you missed and made up.

> *The corporate time-tracking system will not contain enough information to remind you of why you were late to work one day six months ago. This is why it is important for you to keep track of your own time.*

UNACCEPTABLE BEHAVIOR

The previous sections have outlined the basics that will help you make the most out of the relationship you form with your human resources department. Remember, both you and the HR department are working together to achieve the same goal. To ensure a good working relationship with the HR department, keep the following in mind:

- Do not use profane or derogatory language because it could be construed as sexist, racist, ageist or other forms of discrimination.

- Do not make statements or comments that others could take as offensive.

- Do not talk about religion, politics, race, and sexual orientation at work. That includes lunch or other times that you may perceive to be nonwork related.

- When conducting an interview, never ask the interviewee questions about his or her race, religion, age, sexual orientation, or political affiliation.

Being part of an interview is a great experience and a privilege that needs to be taken seriously. This is why it is important for you to seek your HR department's help in acquiring the skills for conducting interviews. Moreover, do your own homework on becoming familiar with the best practices of interviewing so that you do not break any laws.

- Do not send or forward e-mails that contain inappropriate information, that is, e-mails that contain nonwork-related information.

- Do not use the Internet at work for nonwork-related issues, even if your employer permits you to do so. Instead, use your private cell phone to check your private e-mail or websites.

Do not post any offensive information on the Internet or any social media site. Moreover, do not give your coworkers access to your social media sites.

It is legal for employers to review your work e-mails.

Personal Account

After graduating law school, my knowledge of the American legal system gave me a unique insight into the interview process. I encountered companies that understood and ensured laws were not broken during the interview. But I also encountered companies that I think did not realize there are laws that need to be adhered to.

I had an interview after law school that I was very excited about because of the position but it became very clear that the position was not for me because of the interview process. Within the first few minutes, the interviewer—a director level—asked me a question about my religion, which is against the law. The next thing I know this person stopped talking for a few seconds and then started to explain to me that he was sorry because he was distracted by the attractive woman that had just walked by us. This statement was probably illegal on a few grounds but it was also very unprofessional. At that point, I was close to walking out of the interview but I did not. The interview continued and this lack of professionalism also continued. I did not accept the position specifically because of this man's total lack of professionalism.

Companies do monitor what Internet sites their employees visit so you are forewarned.

- Do not wear clothing that others may perceive to be offensive.
- Never make nonwork-related long distance calls at work.
- Never place religious, political, sexual, or racial information in your work area that others may deem offensive.

 The best policy is to place only awards, photos of family and friends, and business-related information in your work area. You want your work area to be an environment in which all people feel comfortable.

Remember, local, personal calls during working hours are acceptable, provided the company has not specifically prohibited this activity, the conversation is limited to five minutes or less, and it does not become a habit.

 If you have to make a personal call, even just to say hello, walk outside and use your cellular phone.

SICK DAYS

A sick day is a day that you do not come to work because you are sick, but you are paid. Sick days were designed by businesses to allow their employees to take time off from work to rest and get well while still getting paid. They want you not only to get better but to ensure that you do not get your coworkers sick. That is a key point that many professionals forget—no matter how much you do not want to take a sick day, you need to ensure that you do not adversely affect your coworkers by working while you are sick. Remember, getting others sick will cause more problems than if you take one or two days off from work to get better. So do not fret about taking a sick day when you are sick because this is what your body needs, your coworkers want, and management needs for you to do.

Prepare for a Sick Day

Read and understand your company's sick day policy. Ensure that you have the necessary information at home on how to report that you are sick. Keep the necessary documentation at home that will allow you to change your voice mail and e-mail notification system to inform others that you are out sick. Maintain a list of contact information for your manager and pertinent coworkers at home or in your personal phone directory.

Do's

- Call in sick when you are sick. Communicate using the proper channels that you are sick in the designated time frame; equally important, ensure that your manager and any pertinent coworkers are informed.

- If possible, leave a professional message on your voice mail that informs callers that you will be out for the day. Enable your e-mail notification that you will be out for the day.

- When you return to work, ensure that you keep track for your own records of when you were sick—along with days that you are late and vacation days.

Don't

- Do not go back to work until you are better and not contagious. Rest and get better! Most important, do not worry or fret over calling in sick. Spend your time getting better not worrying.

Calling in sick because of a hangover is not acceptable and will be frowned on by any business; moreover, coming into work with a hangover is never acceptable.

VACATION TIME

Vacation time is allotted time that you and your business have agreed that you can take off while still being paid. This is time that you use to relax and re-energize so it is important that you take the time off. However, to ensure that you have a relaxing vacation, you need to do the following before and after taking your vacation:

- Request your vacation time at least one month prior to the day.

- Prior to asking your manager for time off, ensure that your coworkers are not taking the same time off as you are requesting. You need to know if it is okay to have more than one team member on vacation at the same time.

- Request vacation time via e-mail to your manager so that there is a record of your manager's affirmation or rejection of your request.

- Save the communication to and from your manager.

Preparation for Vacation Time

Notify your team of your pending vacation time so that they can plan accordingly. Determine who will be your backup during your vacation time. Create a sign to hang on the back of your chair informing people that you are on vacation.

The day before you go on vacation, ensure that you block at least 2 hours during the morning to do the following:

- Review all outstanding e-mails.
- Review all outstanding documents.
- Provide statuses of work to the proper persons.
- Find the instructions to change your voice-mail message.

Voice mail. Change your voice mail to indicate that you are on vacation 1 to 2 hours before you leave for vacation. Make sure that your voice mail indicates how long you will be on vacation and who the caller should contact in case of an emergency. By indicating to only contact the person in case of an emergency will ensure that your backup is not inundated with work that can be looked into once you come back from your vacation.

E-mail. Create an e-mail notification that you will be out of the office. Make sure to include the weekend prior to going on vacation in the days you will be out of office. Furthermore, make sure to spell out specifically the day your vacation starts and ends. Last, it is important to include who your backup is.

E-mail Vacation Notification

To Whom It May Concern:

I am currently on vacation so I am unable to respond to your e-mail until I return to work on 2/13/10; however, if this is an emergency please contact Evan at [phone number/e-mail] who can assist you during my absence.

Vacation Start Day: 1/09/10
Returning to Work: 1/18/10

Thank you,
Adam Scholl

General tasks. Clean your desk prior to going on vacation. Turn off all electronics that are not needed during your absence. Ensure that you say good-bye to all your coworkers. This serves two purposes: one it reminds your coworkers that you will be on vacation and two it shows that you are a team player.

Most important, relax and enjoy your vacation. Do not worry about work while on vacation. Trust me, all your work will be waiting for you when you get back.

PERSONAL ACCOUNT

I have heard story after story of new professionals being afraid to take a vacation because they feared being fired or being laid off from work. Moreover, I have heard many stories of how people worried their entire vacation because they thought they would be fired or reprimanded for a mistake they may or may not have made prior to going on vacation. Trust me, you will not be fired; equally important, things will go wrong whether or not you are on vacation.

The first vacation that I took in my career was to Rome, Italy. The vacation was amazing but I spent a great deal of time worrying that some computer code that I had written prior to the vacation did not work. My worrying was not based on any fact that I knew; it was based more on being insecure in the corporate world.

When I returned to work to my amazement I found out that my code actually did not work! Yes, it did not work; however, I worried for nothing because my professional and seasoned coworkers corrected the problem. Equally important, a coworker went over what I did wrong and explained to me that mistakes occur. So, relax and enjoy your vacation.

Getting Back into the Grind after Your Vacation

The day that you return from your vacation make sure that you arrive thirty minutes early to work for every week that you were on vacation. This will afford you time to review your e-mails and voice mail prior to your manager and coworkers coming into work.

Do's

- Go to your manager and coworkers to say hello. This will get the vacation discussions done on your time and also allow for you to catch up on any business matters that may have occurred.
- Make sure to complete your time reporting for the time you were out on vacation.
- Change your voice-mail message back to the regular message.
- Disable your e-mail notification.
- Plan to stay at work late to make up some of your time spent discussing your vacation with your coworkers.
- Ensure that if you bring any pictures into work that they are appropriate for work. Show them during break time.

PERSONAL TIME

Personal time is time that you spend away from the office during a work day. An example of personal time is when you have to go to the dentist for 1 hour during the day or if you have to go to your child's school play for 2 hours. This is neither sick time nor vacation time so how do you handle these situations? It depends first on your company's policy and then, more importantly, your manager's policy. More likely than not, you can take personal time to do necessary life events but it is important that you do not abuse this policy. Moreover, it is important that you make up any time that you take off.

Do's

Block your calendar that you will be out of the office. Inform your manager by e-mail that you will be out of the office. Most important, notify the coworker(s) that you work closely with where you are going and for how long.

Ensure that you keep your cell phone with you and turned on so that the office can reach you. Remember, this is not a day off so make your errand quick. Document the time that you were away from the office so that you remember to make up the time. Notify your coworkers that you are back in the office.

HOW TO RESIGN FROM YOUR POSITION

There may be a time in your career that you need to leave your position in a company. If this time comes, you need to ensure that you resign from your position properly. This will guarantee that you do not burn any bridges with your company, manager, or coworkers. Remember, the business community is smaller than people realize and leaving a company in a manner that is unprofessional will probably impact you negatively later in your career. Equally important, your letter of resignation will be kept in your company records so you want to ensure that it is professional.

The first step in resigning from your position properly is to create a resignation letter. The letter needs to be short and to the point. The following suggestions will help you create the correct letter:

- Do not write anything negative about your company no matter why you are leaving your position.
- Include a positive note about the company.
- Give at least two-weeks notice.
- Do not state why you are leaving your position unless you are leaving because you are relocating or going back to school.
- Offer to assist in training or replacement or making a transition.
- Specify the last day you will be working.

SAMPLE RESIGNATION LETTER

Date
Name
Address
Phone
E-mail

Dear [Manager's Name]:

Please accept this letter as my resignation from my position as a [position] from [company's name] effective [date]. I have enjoyed working for [company] the last [number] years and leave taking many positive experiences. During this transition period, please let me know if I can be of any help.

Sincerely,

Your Name

The last step in your resignation process is to resign formally. This will be the day that you meet with your reporting manager to resign. It is important to realize that the day you resign may also be the last day you work for the company because the company may not want you to stay for the two-week period. Make sure that you prepare accordingly.

PERSONAL ACCOUNT

I had the greatest learning experience and opportunities at my first career. By the time I was ready to leave my position to obtain my law degree, I had risen up the leadership structure within the organization. This required me to be a leader when I resigned by giving my corporation a six-week notice. I realized that I could not give my corporation a two-week notice because of the short-term void my departure would cause; moreover, I was a stockholder in this company. So, I provided them the longer six-week notice, which I know the firm greatly appreciated. This allowed me to leave the company in good standing professionally and personally.

IN CONCLUSION

The HR department is your friend—not your enemy. Do not be afraid of them; moreover, engage them and use everything they have to offer. Equally important, read and understand your corporate policies so that you do not break any rules. You are a professional so it is your responsibility not only to understand your corporate rules but also the rules and laws for being a part of the business community as a whole.

CHAPTER 7

TIME MANAGEMENT

Lost wealth may be replaced by industry, lost knowledge by study, lost health by temperance or medicine, but lost time is gone forever.

—SAMUEL SMILES

CHAPTER CONCEPTS

What Is Time Management?

Benefits of Effective
Time Management

How to Manage Your Time

WHAT IS TIME MANAGEMENT?

Time management is the term used to describe effectively managing one's time. There are many definitions, flowcharts, theories, and beliefs about time management. Moreover, many chapters and books have been devoted to the subject of time management. But the purpose of this book is to get you started and settled into your career, so it is important to start with a simple, but useful, definition. As your career progresses, you will acquire a greater understanding of how to effectively manage your time. But for now, a basic building block is all that is needed.

Simply put, time management is the process of efficiently and effectively managing your priorities and commitments. This definition requires you to engage in a daily, weekly, and monthly process of determining when your assigned and unassigned work tasks will be completed.

Do not be overwhelmed by this definition because this chapter is devoted to time management. The chapter has two sections: (1) a list of benefits that come from effectively managing your time and (2) a simple time management method. After reading both sections, you will have the basic knowledge to effectively and efficiently manage your time but it is your responsibility as a professional to continue to improve your time management skills.

BENEFITS OF EFFECTIVE TIME MANAGEMENT

There are many benefits to managing your time effectively and efficiently in the corporate world. Once you begin to know and understand these benefits, you will gain a greater appreciation for time management. This appreciation, in turn, will allow you to become an advocate for one of the most important and underdeveloped professional skill sets in the corporate world. The following list describes some of the benefits that result from effective time management:

- Ability to quickly determine when a task cannot be completed within expected time constraints.

- Ability to clearly articulate why you cannot perform a specific task within the allotted time due to your other task commitments.

- Reduction in your levels of stress due to a reliable and well-thought-out daily routine.

- Ability to attach structure and routine to important but largely overlooked tasks, such as reviewing e-mails, furthering educational goals, training, and so on.

- Maintaining balance between your professional and personal life.

- Ability to skillfully balance competing tasks, which in turn allow you sufficient time to produce quality work for every project assigned to you.

- The ability to organize your thoughts, tasks, and deliverables in a manner allowing for forecasts of expected output.

HOW TO MANAGE YOUR TIME

There are many methods and processes for managing your time effectively. I have a simple method that you can use to manage your time. Keep in mind, this method is intended to be a starting point only, just as you are at a starting point in your career. Once you gain a greater appreciation and understanding of time management principles, you will then begin to build on this method. Alternatively, as you progress in your career, you may decide to choose a different method.

The method is broken into eight parts that are easy to understand and manage, which are explained further in this chapter:

1. Identify your tasks.

2. Ensure that your tasks are manageable.

3. Document your tasks.

4. Estimate time required for a task.

5. Prioritize your workload.

6. Plan your workweek.

7. Communicate your workload.

8. Review your work.

Identify Your Tasks

The first step in managing your time is to identify your tasks. This step is relatively easy, provided you remember that absolutely all of your work can be characterized as a task. No matter how small or unimportant a piece of work may appear, it is still a task that needs to be documented and managed. The following table provides an example of tasks that will require your attention in the workplace.

TASKS	
✓ Assigned project tasks	✓ E-mail review and composition
✓ Tracking time spent on work	✓ Corporate education
✓ Job skills development	✓ Mentorship
✓ Corporate, department, and team meetings	✓ Miscellaneous task preparation time

While this list is not intended to be all-encompassing, it is fairly representative of what you will encounter and can be used as a guide for identifying your tasks. Fill in other tasks you have under Others. You will become more comfortable with identifying your tasks as you progress in your career.

Ensuring Your Tasks Are Manageable

Now that you have the ability to identify your tasks, you also need to see to it that your tasks are manageable. By having manageable tasks, you will be able to estimate your work hours. Keep in mind, however, that this step in your time management process is not a science but rather an art form. You will become more efficient at recognizing what tasks are manageable over time, so do not get frustrated. The first question you must ask yourself when you are assigned a task is whether you need to allot more than 40 hours to complete the task.

Assigned Tasks over 40 Hours. If you have been given 40 hours or more to complete an assigned task, then you will need to break the task down into smaller components. This will allow you to forecast future work more precisely, and provide you with a rough framework for organizing your work time more efficiently.

Components of a 40+ Hour Task	
Component	**Actions**
Documentation	E-mails, specific documentation, impromptu memos
Meetings	Small cube meetings, large organized meetings
Research	Issue identification, converse with experts, mentor interaction, information acquisition
Analysis	Perform analysis using collected materials

Assigned Tasks under 40 Hours. If your assigned task has been allotted less than 40 hours of work time for completion, then you do not need to break it down into more manageable tasks.

> A 40-hour task will not be completed in one week because it is expected that employees can devote 32 to 36 hours per week to project work. You will have other administrative and company duties to perform every week.

Document Your Tasks

Now that you have identified your tasks, it will be necessary to track and manage them. This process is not difficult; it is actually easy and sometimes fun. However, before you begin the process, be careful not to overlook the following preliminary steps:

- Choose a software application that can easily manage information such as Microsoft Excel.
- Create a folder in your computer to store your time sheets.
- Be sure to incorporate the appropriate date into your file name when saving a document.

Create a Template. The next phase is to create a template (for an example, the template on page 170) to manage your tasks. The steps in creating a template are:

1. Open a new worksheet in Microsoft Excel (or whichever application you are using).

2. Save the file as your task sheet template in your time sheet folder.

3. At the top of your sheet put two headings: Name and Starting Date.

4. Input the following column headings: Task Name, Completed, Priority, Estimated Start

Task Sheet Template

Name:									
Starting Date:									

TASKS

Task Name	Completed	Priority	Estimated			Actual			Comments
			Start Date	End Date	HRS	Start Date	End Date	HRS	

Date, Estimated End Date, Estimated Hours, Actual Start Date, Actual End Date, Actual Hours, and Comments.

5. Save the file.

You have successfully created your template now let's use it.

Utilize a Task Sheet. Now that your template is complete, it is time for you to apply what you have learned. By following these steps, you will always know what tasks you are working on, what tasks are pending, and what tasks you have recently completed. In addition, by inputting and using this information, you will begin to understand how to estimate task completion times more accurately. By reviewing past estimated dates and hours for specific tasks, you will be able to conceptualize trends in your task progress, allowing you to forecast more accurately. Finally, in keeping with one of the key themes of this book, using a task sheet will bring you one step closer to becoming a professional. Here are the steps you need to follow to prepare a task sheet:

- Make a copy of the template you will use.
- Enter your name and the start date on the task sheet.
- Give your task a name to be used as a reference.
- Put at least the estimated start and end dates even if you are unable to estimate the total hours.

- Enter actual start date, actual end date, and hours worked (when known) into the respective cells.

- Enter any information regarding delays of actual start date, differences between estimate and actual hours, and so on in the comment column.

> *As a result of effectively using a task sheet, you will be able to give quick status reports as needed. By using this simple task sheet, you will have a tremendous amount of useful and reliable information at your fingertips.*

Estimate Time Required for a Task

Accurately estimating the time needed to complete a task is perhaps the most difficult step in the time management process. As this, too, is an art form, the only way to truly master it is through practice. The more often you work at estimating your hours for a given task, the more efficient and effective you will become at making these estimates down the road. While practice does make perfect, there are several important points that will assist you in this process. Here is some basic information to help you start the estimation process.

Task Sheet

Name:	Adam
Starting Date:	July 1

TASKS

Task Name	Completed	Priority	Estimated			Actual			Comments
			Start Date	End Date	HRS	Start Date	End Date	HRS	
020456 Statement of Work	Yes	1	Jul 1	Jul 11	40	Jul 1	Jul 21	60	More detail was needed than expected which required more hours of work.
020456-Business Requirement Document (BRD)	No	1	Jul 14	Nov 14	400	Jul 22			SOW was not approved until 7/21
BRD-Meetings			Jul 14	Nov 14	60	Jul 22			
BRD-Research			Jul 14	Nov 14	80	Jul 22			
BRD-Gather Requirements			Jul 14	Nov 14	100				
BRD-Writing Document			Jul 14	Nov 14	120				
BRD-Review Session			Sep 1	Nov 14	40				

Take a Broad Approach. When estimating your hours for a task, it is very important to think in broad terms. Keep in mind that unexpected things will happen that will require your immediate attention. Thus, when estimating your task completion time, you want to make sure to include time for:

- Meetings
- Documentation
- E-mail
- Research
- Analysis
- Forming your conclusions
- Talking to your mentor

Visualize a Similar Task. Visualize a similar task that you did in college, at a part-time job, at home, and so on. Then break down the components that were part of that task and the time that it took you to complete each component. Use this information to create an estimate for your task.

Ask for Help. View your fellow employees as assets in this process. Thus, ask your mentor or coworker for an estimate. Be sure to inquire how they came up with the estimate; you will need to double their estimated time in order to factor in your inexperience.

Be sure to keep in mind how much time you have been allotted while working on a given task.

Prioritize Your Workload

Prioritizing your workload is a critical component in the time management process. Realistically, it will often be impossible to complete all of your assigned work by the specific target dates. By using strategy and prioritization, you will be able to determine which tasks are the most important so that these tasks are completed ahead of less important projects with less strenuous time deadlines. The following list will help you in prioritizing your work:

- Review your task sheet and calendar to make sure you have enough hours to complete expected work.

- Using critical thinking, determine which project and/or task has priority based on your team and company needs. Review notes, e-mails, and so on to determine what appears to be a priority for the company.

- Take into consideration whether any of your tasks are linked to your coworkers' tasks.

- Determine if any tasks depend on your other tasks.

- Take into consideration if your work is dependent on others completing work first.

> *Unless you are in charge of the overall work effort, you will not be able to make decisions on prioritizing all of your assigned work. However, you should be able to contribute to the discussion.*

Plan Your Workweek

Planning your workweek effectively is essential. When contemplating how you will attack your assigned tasks for a given week, it is very important to plan your workweek because you want to make sure that you manage your time effectively and efficiently. By plotting what tasks will be worked on each day, you will minimize any possible setbacks that could interfere with completing your work.

Communicate Your Workload

Part of the time management process requires you to effectively communicate your workload to your superiors and coworkers. Even though this step is often overlooked by many professionals, it is important because your managers and coworkers will be able to review your estimates, re-prioritize your work, and understand your workload. Hence, again, be a leader by communicating your workload.

Equally important, you will probably have a designated weekly meeting or a requirement for a weekly status report. Both instances are a perfect opportunity to communicate your workload in an organized manner. Make sure to provide a two-week time estimate and be able to provide more detail if you're communicating this information in a meeting. Either way, if you have followed the above steps you can feel assured that you will be able to explain your estimates and prioritizations to anyone who asks.

> *The most important concept to keep in mind is that you must communicate with your manager when you know you cannot possibly complete all the work assigned to you in the given time frame.*

Review Your Work

The final step in managing your time is to review and consider how effective you have been at managing your time. Effective time management is an ongoing process that needs to be continually refined and redefined. Thus, it is important to review the process to determine if improvements need to be made. So make sure to designate at least thirty minutes per month to reviewing your time management process. During this time, analyze whether you followed the rules. Moreover, review your estimates to see if you are improving. The key point is that time management is more than just estimating work; it is a process that is constantly evolving.

Personal Account

Once you can manage your own time, you can use those skills in creating and managing project timelines and also estimating large project tasks. This is a highly sought after ability.

When I worked as a contractor for a Fortune 1000 *company during the summer of my first year in law school, I had the opportunity to showcase my time management skills very early on. I was assigned to help a project incorporate best practices and to educate the staff on these best practices. Very quickly I realized that the project's timelines were very unrealistic. Because this project was sponsored by c-level management, it was important for me to first bring my concerns to lower management and then get their approval to bring my concerns to upper management. With their blessing, I reviewed the requirements of the project and over a two-week period I created a detailed project timeline. I was able to illustrate that the estimated timelines and costs of the* project were unrealistic using my time management process. Moreover, after completing the timeline, I recommended that the project be put on hold because the business expectations were not going to be met.

Subsequently, I was asked to present my findings to management, our business partners, and to one c-level manager. The meeting was tough because of office politics—I was recommending that we stop a project that some people were heavily invested in. However, I stayed above the fray and I let my work product speak for itself. Moreover, I was able to provide specific work experience to back up my estimates when pressed. Management subsequently took my recommendations and implemented them. Moreover, because of this and other work that I had accomplished in a short period of time, I was later offered a full-time position with the company.

IN CONCLUSION

Effective time management is an important part of being a professional. Furthermore, it is an easy process that you will only get better with over time. So it is important that you begin using a time management process early in your career so that you can refine the process in manner that you feel more comfortable with.

CHAPTER 8

OFFICE DYNAMICS

*The ability to deal with people is as purchas-
able a commodity as sugar or coffee and I will
pay more for that ability than for any other
under the sun.*

—JOHN D. ROCKEFELLER

CHAPTER CONCEPTS

The Office

Coworker Friendships

Know Who You Are Talking To

Do Not Be Afraid of
Office Politics

Dealing with
Difficult Coworkers

THE OFFICE

The Office is a television sitcom that revolves around the antics of the manager, Michael, and his staff. I enjoy watching the show because it is funny and it reminds me of—well—the office. I am not saying that all managers are like Michael, but I am saying that all offices do have a Dwight or two or three! *The Office* does a pretty good job of showcasing the dynamics of any office—there are parties that do not go well because people drink, coworkers date and then break up, there are cliques, and gossip, and so on.

In your career, you need to be prepared to adjust to and understand the dynamics of your office because you will be spending so much time there. This is why it is important for you to educate yourself on the different facets of office life. In this chapter I discuss, among other topics, office politics and how to deal with a difficult coworker. These are a just a few facets of working in an office that you need to understand to be a professional. This chapter is not intended to be the end-all on the dynamics of the workplace. Rather, it is intended to raise your awareness and to help you realize its complexity.

COWORKER FRIENDSHIPS

It is part of human nature for us to need companionship. This companionship allows us to feel wanted and needed within the greater human community. This need for companionship does not cease to exist when we walk through the doors of our company. This human requirement is probably more obvious at work because we spend so much time at work; the dynamics of work require professional and personal relationships. However, these relationships need to be carefully crafted into what I have termed *coworker friendships*.

The designation, coworker friendship, signifies that there are certain limits and boundaries that do not exist in your friendships outside of work. A coworker friendship is developed and maintained at work but does not cross over into your personal life. This does not mean you can't go out with your coworkers after work on Friday night for a beer or have dinner with your significant other and a coworker. What it does mean is that you shouldn't speak about specific personal aspects of your life with your coworkers. The list that follows contains subjects that you should not discuss:

- Never speak ill of your significant other or close family members to your friends at work because it shows a lack of loyalty.

- Do not speak about religion or politics because you may offend someone unknowingly and he or she could be your boss sooner than you think.

- Do not speak negatively about your managers or coworkers.

- Do not bash the company for which you work.

- It is not appropriate to speak about crude, rude, or disgusting subjects.

By following these simple guidelines, you will have coworker friendships that will foster your career in the workplace, but not jeopardize it. These friendships will ensure that you have some necessary companionship at work. Furthermore, these guidelines will allow you to progress in your career without worrying that your past actions will come back to haunt you.

If a coworker speaks negatively of another coworker in front of you then first say something nice about that coworker and then change the subject. This lets the person know in a diplomatic way that that you do not intend to talk negatively about others.

PERSONAL ACCOUNT

My parents raised me not to speak ill of others so I carried this life lesson into my professional career. It was difficult in the beginning of my career not to speak ill of others because it is a lot easier to side with the masses than to be a person of change. But my parents encouraged me stick to my virtues because it was the right thing to do and they further explained that professionals stay above the fray. So I stuck to my beliefs and stayed above the fray whenever a coworker spoke negatively about another coworker. Well, a year later during my first performance review I was shocked that eight out of ten of my reviewers detailed how I never spoke ill of anyone and how they perceived this to be a positive trait. Moreover, I remember my manager had highlighted these statements and spoke to me how this is a positive trait of a professional. This is one of many reasons why I have succeeded in my professional career.

KNOW WHO YOU ARE TALKING TO

To function organizations require large numbers of people to work for them. This sometimes results in brothers, friends, cousins, married couples, and extended families working for the same corporation; sometimes coworkers get married and continue to work for the same company. Get to know who is who in the organization. You can do this by asking your boss and coworkers if any of their family members work in the organization. This may help to ensure that you do not say the wrong thing to the wrong person.

Equally important, you need to review the organizational chart so that you know who you are talking to on a hierarchical level. First, you need to find your organizational chart. Second, review the organizational chart while putting a name to a face. Last, practice what you have learned so that you remember who is who. By doing this, you will ensure that you understand the person's position when talking to him or her which is important because you need to understand the authority the person brings to the discussion.

Personal Account

I arrived early for a meeting and began talking to a coworker. She and I were discussing a particular project and I discussed the positive things about the program manager on the project. I distinctly remember talking in detail about how well this program manager had handled a problem with an employee; moreover, how impressed I was with this program manager. After working two years at the company, I found out that the program manager and the coworker were cousins.

It is also important for you to understand your company's organizational chart because it will have an impact on your career. For example, let's say that you work in the information technology department in your company. Furthermore, the head of that department is not designated as the CIO but instead is an executive that reports to the CFO. The structure requires the information technology department to get approval for projects from the CFO first before the president gets involved. This means that the information technology department has to first get approval from a finance expert who is not a technological expert before the requests are presented to the president of the company. This added layer can cause disruptions and delays within the information technology department that will affect your ability to advance as a professional. The key point to remember is that decisions made at the top can and will affect your career.

DO NOT BE AFRAID OF OFFICE POLITICS

Make no mistake about it: You will encounter office politics. More likely than not, you probably hold a negative view of office politics. It has taken me a considerable amount of time in both the corporate and academic worlds to develop a full understanding and appreciation of office politics. You may be surprised to learn that office politics isn't all negative.

First, I define office politics as the perceived internal (true or false) hierarchal power structure that simultaneously emboldens and hinders people in achieving a desired objective. The hierarchy will be fragmented within the corporate structure. For instance, there will be a hierarchy among the secretaries that may extend to the managers. Or the managers may have their own hierarchy that could include the vice-president's secretary. Either way it is important to realize that this perceived power structure spans all departments. Equally important, this power structure is intended to ensure the status quo. People want to ensure that they have a *job*—I did not say a career because people mixed in office politics are not professionals and therefore lack the understanding that office politics are not necessary to succeed as a professional.

Second, office politics should not be viewed as a single action but as a never-ending series of actions that foster this perceived hierarchal power structure. The actions of others create the dynamics of office politics. Moreover, the continued actions of others foster it by either contributing directly or indirectly to the never-ending cycle.

Third, whether you like it or not, office politics are here to stay. So, rather than running away from it, face it head-on and deal with it. Hence, it is important that you understand that it exists in some shape or form at each and every company and that you will need to deal with it sooner or later. However, this does not mean you have to play office politics. You just need to realize that it exists so that you do not fall victim to it.

Last, office politics can be good for a corporation; it just depends on how it is used and, more importantly, by whom. Sometimes office politics can be used to foster positive change within a business environment. However, it is important to understand the dynamics of the company's office politics and have a plan of exit before using it for positive change. As a professional, it is important to realize the potential of all tools for the future even though you may not be in a position to use office politics yet.

Do not fear office politics. It is not always bad and it exists ubiquitously in every organization. However, it is your job to ensure that you do not become entangled in your organization's office politics. Equally important, it is your job to be a professional and to rise above the fray.

*Buy a copy of **Who Moved My Cheese?** and read it. Moreover, keep the copy at your desk and let people (this includes yourself) read it when the time is necessary. You will know when the time is right.*

PERSONAL ACCOUNT

I have been able to use office politics as an agent of change. For example, I was asked to provide guidance on how to implement new guidelines and processes in a fast-moving environment. I was informed that other people in the company had already tried to implement these changes previously to no avail. I realized quickly that the power structure (i.e., office politics) stopped this change out of fear because they did not understand that the changes were needed and beneficial. So I knew that I had to get buy in from these de facto leaders. I devised a strategy where I made these leaders part of the implementation process, which made them a partner of the change. Through experience I knew that they would get their friends (coworkers) to embrace the change, which they did. This is an example where experience and an understanding of office politics led to a win-win for all.

DEALING WITH DIFFICULT COWORKERS

The most difficult part of your career (or any job for that matter) is dealing with coworkers. Your coworkers are just like you: they have problems, significant others, medical appointments, bad days, health issues, children, deaths in the family, and other problems that do not go away when they walk through the door to work.

It is important for you to remember that your coworkers are people and are therefore by definition, complex. This complexity mandates that you be patient while effectively managing situations.

Not all people are meant to be in the business world. That is just a fact. Trust me, I have worked with and for many people who should do all of us a favor and pick another career in the public sector.

As a professional you will have to deal with difficult coworkers. Dealing with them is not easy and will require all the tools from your tool belt. It is important for you to continue educating yourself on this subject because the more responsibility you gain in your career the more often you will be involved in dealing with difficult coworkers. Here is a four-step process on how to deal with difficult coworkers:

1. **State the problem.** You need to write down what problem or problems you are having with a coworker in a nonconfrontational manner. Moreover, make sure that your statements are short and concise.

2. **Review the problem.** Review your problems 24 hours later. This will give you time to reflect and to verify that you have stated the problems correctly. Equally important, make sure that the problems you stated are not self-correcting. If they are then correct yourself by creating a short-term goal.

3. **Discuss the problem.** This will be the difficult part of the process but it is the most important step. If you believe that you cannot discuss the matter with the person alone then seek your supervisor's help in mediating the discussion with the person. However, if you believe that you can talk to the person one-on-one then do so. Make sure that you start the conversation on a positive note by saying that you enjoy working with the person for specific reasons. Then proceed into why you wanted to talk to them. It is important that you talk to the person in a nonconfrontational manner. Equally important, listen to what the person has to say and do not become defensive. Remember, you are meeting with the person to solve a problem that is affecting the company and your performance.

4. **Recap.** Immediately after meeting with the person, recap the meeting in writing so that you do not forget what occurred. Review your meeting notes the following day to determine if you need to add any further information. Save the document so that if the problem persists you have a record of the correcting actions that you have tried to take. Also, it is important that you do not discuss the meeting you had with the difficult coworker with any of your other coworkers. This meeting was between you and the other person; so keep it that way.

These steps provide a starting point on how to deal with difficult coworkers. It is your responsibility to continue to educate yourself on this subject because it is a complex process that will require courage, strength, and leadership. It is also an important part of managing people, something all professionals will do to varying degrees.

> Take the time to read **How to Win Friends and Influence People** by Dale Carnegie.
> This classic book, written in 1937, is as useful today as when it was first written.

IN CONCLUSION

The workplace is a fluid environment that requires you to be patient and professional at all times. It is important to stay above the fray and be a professional. You can do this by not being part of the office politics and by having coworker friendships. Moreover, make sure to deal with difficult coworkers as soon as possible so the situation does not affect your work. This is your career, so be smart.

> **Office Space** is a movie that I highly recommend.
> It provides some great insights on the dynamics of the workplace.

CHAPTER 9

PUTTING IT ALL TOGETHER . . .

Now that you have read the entire book, it is time to put it all together. There were many principles, concepts, anecdotes, and examples provided in this book that were derived from my corporate experience and education. It was presented to you with the intention of providing you with the necessary tools—business practices and principles—to successfully manage your first few years in the corporate world and to create a solid professional business knowledge base. Here is a brief summary of what we covered:

The Corporate Look. As a professional, it is always important that you look professional so that you are taken seriously. By always looking professional, you ensure that your work product is judged—not your appearance. Dress for the position that you want.

Professionalism in Communication. It is important that you communicate in a professional manner. This includes e-mails, memos, phone conversations, presentations, and so on. Make sure that your message is concise and short so that you keep your audience's attention.

Meetings. Meetings are an essential component of the business process so it is important to know your role and what is expected of you. Moreover, it is important to take meetings seriously because they can become a source of wasted time. Furthermore, while you will not be a facilitator in your first week, it is important to start understanding what is expected of a facilitator now so that you are prepared when the time comes for you to assume this important role.

Traveling for Work. Traveling for your company will most likely be part of your duties so make the best of the time. Taking the necessary time to plan and prepare for your trip will ensure that you have a successful trip. While traveling for your company, remember that you always represent it so be professional at all times.

Career Growth. This is your career so you need to manage it now. Start tracking your progress so that you know your strengths and weaknesses. Equally important, it is your responsibility to continue to educate yourself within your discipline. Remember, it is not okay to expect to educate yourself just on your company's time, you must continue to expand your knowledge base outside of designated work time.

Human Resources. The HR department is your friend not your enemy so utilize all of the resources they have to offer. Moreover, never act inappropriately, this way the HR department will always be your advocate.

Time Management. Understanding and practicing time management is a key component of being a professional. This is why I provided a process for you to use to effectively manage your time. So either use the process that was provided in this book or another process. Just be sure to use one.

Office Dynamics. One of the toughest aspects of being a professional is confronting difficult coworkers in a professional manner. Even though it is tough, it will not only benefit you professionally but also personally as the discomfort that you experience in dealing with these types of people will diminish.

Now it is time for you to put to use what you have learned in this book in your professional career. All the material in this book bundled together is another tool in your tool belt. This means that you have an extra tool that you can grab any time you need to manage your time, deal with a difficult coworker, communicate in a professional manner, and so on. However, all tools are not built the same and all tools eventually need to be replaced. It is your responsibility to continue to read and educate yourself so that your tool belt continues to expand with more tools. And that is the key to being a professional. It is that simple—continue to educate yourself so that you have the right tools to deal with any issue.

Good luck and I look forward to meeting you at the office.

Index

R

S